I highly recommend this book to girls for a daily or weekly devotional-like read. It's jam-packed with wisdom, reality, and a whole lot of fun. High-five to Susie and Kristin. . .and to every girl who reads it!

HOLLY STARR
NATIONAL RECORDING ARTIST AND WORSHIP LEADER

Susie and Kristin have hit on just about any topic a teen girl can think up and given sound advice. This is the kind of book every young woman needs to have on her shelf.

ANNIE DOWNS
AUTHOR OF *SPEAK LOVE AND PERFECTLY UNIQUE*

This book contains fun, practical, and wise advice every girl should hear. Susie and Kristin give awesome advice for girls. I'm even making my three-year-old read it!

KERRI POMAROLLI
COMEDIAN AND AUTHOR OF *GUYS LIKE GIRLS NAMED JENNIE*

Susie and Kristin cover almost any topic that a parent would want their teen daughter to hear about. They'll tell your daughter what you're telling her. . .and she'll believe them. It's just how it works.

DANNAH GRESH
BESTSELLING AUTHOR AND CREATOR OF SECRET KEEPER GIRL

I love that Kristin is a young, hip, funny comedian offering my daughter godly advice. Having my daughter read daily from these charming and entertaining insights instead of listening to me blurt out some nonsense is going to be far more effective for those awkward subjects like how to best cover up your three *B*s. Get the book to determine exactly what those three *B*s are!

MARTY SIMPSON
2012 CLEAN COMEDY CHALLENGE WINNER, FATHER OF ONE TEENAGE DAUGHTER

Smart Girl's GUIDE

TO GOD, GUYS, AND THE GALAXY

SAVE THE DRAMA! AND 100 OTHER PRACTICAL TIPS FOR TEENS

Susie Shellenberger & KRISTIN WEBER

SHILOH RUN PRESS

To Linda Comingdeer.
Thanks for helping me
make some very smart choices.

—Susie

· · · · · · · · · · · · · · · · · ·

To my family.
You know who you are.
—Kristin

· · · · · · · · · · · · · · ·

Contents

1.

If someone gossips to you, they'll gossip about you.

Think about it. If someone is willing to say nasty things *to* you about someone else, what makes you think they won't say mean things *about* you to others?

Gossip is talking about things that aren't confirmed to be true, don't matter, or aren't any of your business. Gossip usually ends up hurting someone.

"Did you see the way Amber looked at that new guy today? She's totally into him."

How do you know she's totally into him? Did Amber *tell* you this? If not, don't talk about it. Maybe the new guy happened to be standing in front of the clock, and she wanted to know the time.

"Did you see what Sally was wearing? Her family must shop at the tacky barn!"

Why does it matter what Sally wears? Does it affect her more substantial qualities like her **personality**, character, or intellect? No, it doesn't. Also, if there were a place called the Tacky Barn selling clothes, I'd be there every day.

Here's the thing: Gossip is **easy**. It's not difficult to find fault in people. Everyone's riddled with flaws, including you. As Christians, though, we're supposed to **build up**, not **tear down**.

When a conversation turns toward gossip there's **nothing** wrong with gently calling it out by saying, "Hey, I'm trying not to gossip. Do you mind if we change the subject? Did you see the new slide opened at the water park? It looks crazy!"

This is a **polite** way of getting the subject changed and maybe the start of a trip to the water park. If you can't defend a person who is being talked badly about, excuse yourself from the conversation.

If you're around people who constantly tear into others, it may be time to start hanging around a different group of people.

It's also really easy to gossip when someone hurts or offends you. If a brother or sister in Christ upsets you, the Bible tells us to go **directly** to that person and **tell them** they've hurt you. (Do it nicely. Don't scream it in their face.) Give them a chance to apologize, and **be ready to forgive**. It's not easy, but it's **much, much** less hurtful than "venting," exaggerating, or spreading rumors through gossip. If you need advice on how to handle a situation, go to a **parent, youth pastor, or**

mentor and get their perspective. This is different than gossiping about it with your friends.

Sometimes we're so used to gossip it's hard to think of other things to talk about. Good conversation takes effort. It requires **thought, knowledge**, and **understanding**. Sometimes conversation means saying nothing at all and simply **listening**.

Need some conversation ideas? Start with **asking** about the other person's day. **Tell them** about your day. **Talk about** what's going on in your community. **Talk about God** and what He's doing in your life. Let the conversation go from there! You'll be surprised at how **fun** and **enjoyable** it is.

Happy conversing!

Kristin

• •

FROM GOD:

💙 "Keep your tongue from evil and your lips from telling lies" (Psalm 34:13 NIV).

💙 "From the same mouth come blessing and cursing. My brothers, these things ought not to be so" (James 3:10 ESV).

GO AHEAD—ANSWER:

»——→ Are you guilty of gossip? What makes gossip so easy?

»——→ Have you ever been hurt by gossip? Why is gossip so hurtful?

»——→ What are some other things you can talk about besides other people?

FROM KRISTIN:

Sometimes the only thing we have in common with someone is what we gossip about. You may need to reevaluate some friendships or find other common ground to talk about. P.S. Go read all of James 3, which talks about taming the tongue.

FROM SUSIE:

I heard Kristin saves her gum and chews it the next day.

2.
Treat your parents with respect, even if you don't think they deserve it.

It's funny how **smart** parents suddenly become when you get to be around twenty-two years of age. Usually around the time students graduate from **college**, they begin to realize their parents actually know what they're talking about. This is also around the time that your relationship with Mom and Dad begins **transforming** from parent/child to parent/friend. It's an exciting transition. It doesn't happen overnight. And it's usually a **process**. But it often begins around your early to mid-twenties.

But what about now?

Though it may *seem* like your folks don't know what they're talking about, they usually do. Unless you've been hired by the CIA to create a brand-new code that enables you and your friends to leave the house at midnight while your parents are sort of frozen-but-still-conscious and can't move as you walk right past them and take the family car to pick up your friends and head to Dairy Queen even though it's closed but your secret code allows you inside and you make chocolate malts for everyone, fire up the grill, flip some burgers, use a lot of cheese, and come back home and go to bed and the next morning when you see your parents at breakfast and they say, "We know what's happening. We're frozen, and we can't move when it happens, but we know you have a secret code. And guess what! We've cracked the code. You're not going to Dairy Queen anymore until you're forty-six!" In this case, your parents probably really *don't* know what they're talking about because, remember, the CIA are the ones who have hired you to create this code and if they've hired you, you totally know they've protected the code and probably have bodyguards wearing invisible suits protecting you on the way to Dairy Queen and back and there's no way your parents have actually cracked the code but even though they really *don't* know what they're talking about in this particular situation it would still be wise to respect them or else you'll end up writing run-on sentences about ridiculous scenarios and codes that will never exist.

Right now is a great time to build on the foundation you and your folks need to have to make the transition from parent/child to parent/friend someday. Let them know you're trustworthy. When you disagree, ask if you can discuss the issue instead of screaming, "You're so unfair! Jasmine's parents let HER bungee off the Golden Gate Bridge!"

Most parents are **overworked** and underpaid. Do something today to make your mom's life **easier**. Think of a way you can **encourage** your dad. Clean the house without being asked. Have dinner ready for them tonight. Learn to be a **peacemaker** in your home. And practice love—lots of it.

What does it actually mean to **respect** your parents? **Give** them the benefit of the doubt. Be **obedient** (you'll be amazed at how far this will get you once you get out into the work world!). **Listen** to them. Be kind.

The more you respect your parents now, the greater your relationship will be when you make the transition!

Susie

• •

FROM GOD:

❤ "My son, keep your father's command and do not forsake your mother's teaching" (Proverbs 6:20 NIV).

❤ "A fool spurns a parent's discipline, but whoever heeds correction shows prudence" (Proverbs 15:5 NIV).

GO AHEAD—ANSWER:

»⟶ In what two areas do you and your parents have the most conflict?

»⟶ Discuss three things you can do to make the conflict better.

»⟶ What are some specific things you can do to show respect to your parents?

FROM SUSIE:

Do your parents insist on giving you a curfew, going to church as a family, knowing who your friends are, and praying for you? If so, celebrate! They're in the process of giving you a strong heritage that will last a lifetime. When you're twenty-two, you'll actually thank them.

FROM KRISTIN:

Parents have been charged by God to raise their children to love Him and teach them to follow His commands. This is a huge responsibility—so cut them some slack if they seem overbearing or overprotective. You'll understand when you're a parent yourself one day.

3.
Study the Bible

"I just don't understand it."

"It's out of date."

"I get bored."

"I just can't make myself do it."

If you've caught yourself making any of the above excuses about why you don't read the Bible, you're not alone. Lots of teens have trouble reading the Bible, but it **doesn't have to be this way!**

Think of the Bible as God's personal love letter to you. The Bible is a book filled with **adventure**, mystery, love, war, romance, poetry, surprise, promise, and **hope**. It's reported as the most printed and distributed book in the world.

It provides guidance, wisdom, truth, and instruction. The more we read and study it, the better we get to know God. Reading and studying the Bible also helps us learn to know God's voice. Some teens say, "God never talks to me."

My response is, "How often do you read the Bible?"

"Well, not a lot."

"How do you expect to learn God's voice if you're not reading His letter and learning about Him?"

Have you ever read a **favorite book** so much that you feel you actually know the characters? The same thing happens when you fall in love with reading the Bible. You get to know the people inside—but more importantly, you get to know the God behind it all.

And when you start memorizing scripture, the **Holy Spirit** will bring it to your mind exactly when you need it! Seriously. That's part of His job description.

So let's say you're totally in **knots** about something in your life. If you've memorized 2 Corinthians 4:8–9, the Holy Spirit will bring it to your mind, and you'll be able to rest in its truth.

"We are pressed on every side by troubles, but not crushed and broken. We are perplexed because we don't know why things happen as they do, but we don't give up and quit. We are hunted down, but God never abandons us. We get knocked down, but we get up again and keep going" (TLB).

But it takes more than simply *reading* the Bible for it to make the kind of difference in your life that you want it to. **Studying** and memorizing some of it are also important.

Go to your local Christian bookstore and look at several youth Bibles. Flip through the pages and look at the graphics. Are they easy to follow? Look at the study notes. Do you understand them? What kind of extras does it offer: questions and answers, fiction scenarios, historical background, illustrations, red letters, easy-to-read print?

Look up one of your **favorite** scripture verses in several different versions. Which one is easiest for you to understand? For example, let's look at 1 Timothy 4:12 in a few different versions:

"Don't let anyone think little of you because you are young. Be their ideal; let them follow the way you teach and live; be a pattern for them in your love, your faith, and your clean thoughts" (TLB).

"Don't let anyone look down on you because you are young, but set an example for the believers in speech, in conduct, in love, in faith and in purity" (NIV).

"Let no one look down on your youthfulness, but rather in speech, conduct, love, faith and purity, show yourself an example of those who believe" (NASB).

"Let no one despise your youth, but be an example to the believers in word, in conduct, in love, in spirit, in faith, in purity" (NKJV).

Take your time **searching** through the variety of student Bibles on the shelves. There are lots available! Get a Bible you're proud of and one you can easily understand. If it's too expensive, put it on your birthday or Christmas wish list. And once you get it, carry it with you proudly and delve into reading, studying, and memorizing.

Then start marking it up!

Yes, Bibles are for marking up. If you don't understand something, put a question mark by that verse so you can ask someone about it later. Underline verses that are special to you. Mark those you want to memorize.

Maybe you're thinking, *This sounds good, but I just don't have time to read the Bible.*

This is one of the most important disciplines you'll ever establish in your entire life! Make it a **habit** to read your Bible one minute a day. You can do that. And after you've done a minute each day for a while, you'll be surprised at how you're now doing it five minutes, then ten minutes, and how you begin to *yearn* for more time to read it.

The Bible is our spiritual food. Just as you can't be physically healthy without **nourishment**, neither can you be spiritually healthy without reading the Bible. Here's an exciting goal: strive to read through the entire Bible in one year.

It's easier than you think! If you'll simply read three chapters each day and read five chapters each Sunday, you'll automatically have the Bible finished in one year. **Try it!**

Susie

FROM GOD:

♥ "The whole Bible was given to us by inspiration from God and is useful to teach us what is true and to make us realize what is wrong in our lives; it straightens us out and helps us do what is right. It is God's way of making us well prepared at every point, fully equipped to do good to everyone" (2 Timothy 3:16–17 TLB).

♥ "Man shall not live on bread alone, but on every word that comes from the mouth of God" (Matthew 4:4 NIV).

GO AHEAD—ANSWER:

»—→ Do you have a life verse—a scripture you've decided to adapt for yourself—one to build your life upon? If so, share it with someone. If not, ask God to help you select one.

»—→ In what ways would your life be different if you read the Bible every day?

»—→ Will you find someone to hold you accountable in reading the Bible daily?

FROM SUSIE:

I used to have a pastor who encouraged us to read through the Bible each year, so I tried to read a different version each year. It was exciting. One year I decided to read through the Bible on my knees. What an incredible year that was!

FROM KRISTIN:

Try reading passages from a certain angle. For example, read through Psalms and specifically look for references to how God reveals His love.

4.
Dream big.

How big? As big as the sky. Outta this world! Dream big because you have a **giant** of a God who dreams BIG for **you!** In fact, He dreams bigger for you than you would ever dream for yourself. And He always calls you to something bigger . . .something **beyond** yourself.

Why? Because if it were within your grasp, you wouldn't need Him. But when the dream is bigger than you can imagine, or when it involves a miracle, or it's just outside your reach, you'll depend on Him.

Here's even **more** exciting news: God plants His **God-sized** dreams inside your **heart!** So if you're living in the center of His will, His desires become your desires. And guess what He has promised? According to Psalm 37:4, "Take delight in the Lord, and he will give you the desires of your heart" (NIV).

Let's take a peek at a few young people who have dared to dream big:

- Katie Davis. She wrote the book *Kisses from Katie: A Story of Relentless Love and Redemption.* This is an amazing story of a nineteen-year-old girl who planned on spending a year in Uganda, Africa, before she entered college. But God's desires became her desires. She ended up moving there, falling in love with the children and the country, and is now a mom to kids who will be forever changed because of her love. Check out her blog: kissesfromkatie.blogspot.com.

- Bella. At age sixteen she wanted a car but obviously needed lots of money. So she launched her own jewelry biz. Three years later, Origami Owl is exploding. Google them. Great jewelry! Way to dream big, Bella.

- Zach Hunter was only twelve when he discovered that slavery wasn't just a subject inside his history book. He began studying human rights and got angry enough to make a difference. There are 27 million people who are still trapped in slavery. Maybe you've read one of his four books or are familiar with his campaign Loose Change to Loosen Chains. Zach is simply following the dream placed in his heart by God.

- Ayna Agarwal loves animals. In fact, she loves them so much she launched SPOT Globally—an international organization that helps stop the overpopulation of animals. She educates communities around the world about the danger of untreated animals staying with humans.

Those are just a few of hundreds of students who dared to dream big, follow the desire of their hearts, and trust God to do the rest. What could He do through you. . .if you dared to **dream beyond** yourself and totally trust Him?

Susie

• •

FROM GOD:

❤ "Now glory be to God—who by his mighty power at work within us is able to do far more than we would ever dare to ask or even dream of—infinitely beyond our highest prayers, desires, thoughts, or hopes" (Ephesians 3:20 TLB).

❤ " 'I say this because I know what I am planning for you,' says the LORD. 'I have good plans for you, not plans to hurt you. I will give you hope and a good future' " (Jeremiah 29:11 NCV).

GO AHEAD—ANSWER:

»—→ Do you have a dream to make a difference? Describe it.

»—→ What could keep you from making your dream reality?

»—→ How can your dream become reality?

FROM SUSIE:

I have confidence in dreaming big because I serve a BIG God!

5.
Have guy "friends" not boyfriends.

Have you ever wondered why **some** people have lots of friends? They seem to be people magnets—others are just drawn to them. It's because they've learned an important secret: **Be nice to everyone!** Making friends isn't rocket science; neither is having good friendships with guys. **The problem?** Most girls are so focused on finding a boyfriend, they overlook the obvious: guys make great **friends!**

Lydia was one of **those girls** who had learned the secret. She always said hi to guys and sometimes plopped down at their table in the lunchroom, but she never followed them or made them feel like she was after them. She became a good friend with several of them.

And why is this important? It gave her confidence in learning how to interact with the opposite sex, asking good questions, carrying on an interesting conversation, and caring about them as she would any friend.

When guys could see that she genuinely **cared** and wasn't chasing them, they accepted her and enjoyed her friendship.

Haley, on the other hand, was guy-crazy. She knew which guys had what lunch period, where each one sat, and their class schedule. Haley wanted a boyfriend **so bad**, she was willing to do almost anything. Guess what! Guys know when a girl feels desperate. And the kind of guy who will take advantage of a desperate girl is **not** the kind of guy you want!

Haley wrote notes to guys, followed them, texted them. . .and was just always around. **Most guys** weren't interested in her because she was too desperate. She placed too much emphasis on getting a boyfriend out of the deal. Lydia, however, simply went with the flow. If a guy didn't say hi to her one day, **it was okay**. She didn't let it bother her. But Haley's entire day would be ruined.

Why is it more important to have good guys friends instead of boyfriends? It won't always be this way, but during the *teen* years, you're still learning how to act and react around guys; you're still absorbing **social etiquette**. And some girls have so many boyfriends that they have a difficult time staying in a committed relationship once they become older. They're so used to **ending a relationship** and moving on to the next one that when they get married, they see leaving as the best solution when things don't go perfectly.

It's natural to have friends of the opposite sex when you're a teen. It gets out of hand when you become obsessed. So concentrate simply on being **nice** to everyone and developing good guy friends. Be content to leave it at that. **In His perfect timing**, God will do the rest. You really **can** trust Him!

Susie

• •

FROM GOD:

♥ "The righteous choose their friends carefully, but the way of the wicked leads them astray" (Proverbs 12:26 NIV).

♥ "A friend loves at all times" (Proverbs 17:17 NKJV).

GO AHEAD—ANSWER:

»—→ Is it important to have friends of the opposite sex?

»—→ Do you want to be known as a guy chaser or simply someone who knows how to be a great friend?

»—→ What happens to the stress of having a boyfriend when you decide to simply be a friend to everyone?

FROM SUSIE:

I'm grateful for the male friends in my life who help me change hard-to-reach lightbulbs in my ceiling, carry heavy things for me, and give me good ideas for my lawn.

6.
Malls are overrated.

Go for a hike, see a play, or put together a fund-raiser for your church's missions. Just do *something* besides hanging for hours around an indoor fountain that has water dyed blue to make it look more like water.

I have a personal bias on this one. Personally, I **loathe** malls. The **overwhelming** combination of linoleum, recessed lighting, food-court smells, and mannequins makes me want to curl up in a fake department store bed and take a **long nap**.

My **mall cynicism** launched into overdrive, however, when I realized that one mall fountain had dyed the water blue. (The water apparently failed at looking like water so they had to give it a little makeover.)

For the sake of fairness I'll try to set my bias aside and make my case against malls logically and objectively.

- With the exception of outdoor shopping centers, malls deprive you of fresh air.
- Browsing reminds you of all the things you don't own and fosters discontentment.
- Shopping for clothing is painful and agonizing. (This might be personal. I have no fashion sense and a body shape that works best in a burlap sack.)

I understand the necessity for malls in our culture: they're a way to get everything you need in one place, harking back to the days when people traveled to one big market to get everything they needed. The **key word** in the previous sentence, by the way, is *needed*. Unfortunately we live in a **consumer-driven** society where companies try and convince you that you need more than you do.

Many a decent hour has been lost to people meandering through malls, bemoaning things they can't afford and wasting money on things they don't need.

Instead of wandering around stores aimlessly, **go to malls with a purpose**. Take a list of things you **need** to get, people you **need** to buy for, and specific stores where you can find these **needed** items.

Use the time and money you save to do something more productive. Go for a bike ride, volunteer at your church, or grab some friends and go hike by the lake—I'm pretty sure the water there is allowed to be itself.

Kristin

FROM GOD:

- ♥ "Keep your life free from love of money, and be content with what you have, for he has said, 'I will never leave you nor forsake you' " (Hebrews 13:5 ESV).
- ♥ "For all that is in the world—the desires of the flesh and the desires of the eyes and pride of life—is not from the Father but is from the world" (1 John 2:16 ESV).

GO AHEAD—ANSWER:

- »→ Do you buy what you need, or do you buy excess stuff that makes you feel better?
- »→ When do you find yourself shopping? When you're happy? Sad? When your clothes are so old they're disintegrating off of you?
- »→ Are material possessions an idol for you?

FROM KRISTIN:

One time I went to a mall that had two of the same store on opposite ends of the building. I wandered around the parking lot for almost an hour looking for my car only to realize I had parked outside the other store. I'm still struggling to forgive whoever designed that mall.

FROM SUSIE:

I love malls. In fact, I lived in one until I was twenty-four. Every winter when the birds migrated south, I'd head down to Sears.

FROM KRISTIN:

That's not true.

FROM SUSIE:

I know. I was just trying to be funny.

FROM KRISTIN:

Just keep writing. We have a book to finish.

FROM SUSIE:

I'll work on it later. I'm headed to the mall for an Orange Julius.

7.

Dress fashionably, but modestly.

You want to be remembered for your personality (which is unique), not your cleavage (which looks exactly like everyone else's).

What do you **think** about when you get dressed in the morning?

Do you dress for **comfort**? Do you wait till the **last minute** and simply grab the first clean thing you can find? Or do you pick something that will direct people's attention to your body?

Be honest.

Every society has **different** fashion standards. Even different cities within the same country have varying styles based on climate, culture, and other factors.

Maybe you've been told to wear shorts that come to your fingertips. Or to stay away from tank tops. If you live in a **hot** climate or have really long arms and legs (like me!), it can be tough to find cute clothes that fit modest standards. Tough. But **not** impossible. Think about your clothing choices because **modesty matters**.

First, your outward appearance should be a **reflection** of what Christ is doing in your **heart**. If Christ is transforming you, then your entire life—including what you wear—should reflect that transformation.

"Do not be conformed to this world, but be transformed by the renewal of your mind" (Romans 12:2 ESV).

Don't dress immodestly just because it's the trend. That's conforming to the world. As Christ renews your mind, you'll see that your outer appearance is a way of expressing God's work in your life.

Secondly, dress modestly out of respect for others. God created males to respond to physical beauty. In other words, guys are extremely visual. This is a **good** thing for your *future*. You want your husband to find you **attractive**. But what about *now*?

The way you dress can cause guys to start thinking about you in ways that are improper and impure. Christian guys are fighting to keep their minds pure. Dressing modestly is a way of respecting and honoring the way **God made them**.

Finally, dressing modestly reminds us that our physicality is not the most important aspect of our existence. Television, magazines, and society will tell you that you have to look a **certain way** (usually by buying *their* product) and that staying young and beautiful is super important if you want to feel loved.

Our physical bodies will pass away. Our souls will not. **God wants** you to put more time into developing your **character** than your outward appearance. These traits have eternal value.

"Charm is deceitful, and beauty is vain, but a woman who fears the LORD is to be praised" (Proverbs 31:30 ESV).

It's not wrong to look your best. Learn to apply makeup wisely. Use it to **enhance** your natural beauty—not to cover it up. Go ahead—make an appointment with a great hair stylist and get a cut that accentuates the shape of your beautiful face.

It's an amazing thing when your **character** shines from within and actually complements your style! Inner beauty is more valuable than passing and fleeting fashion fads! (Try saying "fleeting fashion fads" five times fast.)

You can still dress fashionably without having your cleavage, booty, or stomach hanging out. Modesty doesn't mean you need to wear a **burlap sack** to school or a **neoprene jumper** to the beach.

Look at different fashions and figure out a way to wear them modestly. If you like a low-cut shirt, wear a camisole underneath. Pants too tight? Tie a scarf around your waist or use a larger shirt and bunch it in the middle with a belt. This is your chance to use your **creativity** and **unique style**!

Before you leave the house, take a moment to make sure your outfit doesn't draw attention to the *three Bs*: boobs, butt, and belly. (Did I just make you feel awkward? Sorry!) Make sure those are (a) covered and (b) not skintight.

If you're not sure if something is appropriate, ask your **parents**, sister, or trusted friend (not a guy friend).

Kristin

• •

FROM GOD:

❤ "Do not let your adorning be external—the braiding of hair and the putting on of gold jewelry, or the clothing you wear—but let your adorning be the hidden person of the heart with the imperishable beauty of a gentle and quiet spirit, which in God's sight is very precious" (1 Peter 3:3–4 ESV).

❤ "I want women to show their beauty by dressing in appropriate clothes that are modest and respectable. Their beauty will be shown by what they do, not by their hair styles or the gold jewelry, pearls, or expensive clothes they wear" (1 Timothy 2:9 GWT).

GO AHEAD—ANSWER:

»——→ Think about what you wear. What does your outward appearance say about your heart?

»——→ How can you dress modestly and fashionably? Share some specific ideas.

»——→ What differences would you see if you spent as much time in the Word as you do getting dressed?

FROM KRISTIN:

To me, comfort is of key importance when picking out what you're going to wear for the day. It just so happens that modest clothes are often the most comfortable! Coincidence? I think not!

8.

Honor God with your time and talents.

There's an old movie based on a true story called *Chariots of Fire* about a Christian runner named Eric Liddell. A naturally gifted sprinter, Liddell makes it all the way to the Olympics. When explaining his decision to run competitively, Eric uses the following famous quote:

"I believe God made me for a purpose. . .but He also made me fast, and when I run I feel God's pleasure."

God gave each of us a specific set of gifts and talents, and we need to steward our time and talents in a way that honors God.

First, you can use your time and talents to support the church, both **local** and **worldwide**. Are you a good singer? **Sing** on the praise and worship team. Are you great with kids? **Volunteer** in the nursery. Do you love to bake? Join the **hospitality** team.

Second, you can honor God with your gifts **outside** church. Simply doing what God made you to do glorifies Him. He gave you those talents to be salt and light in the world. Pursuing your gifts can take you to unique situations that allow you to share the gospel.

If God **gifted** you in music, practicing diligently and performing your best in the school orchestra brings Him glory. If you're **skilled** at organizing, helping your student council plan events brings Him glory. If you're an athlete, playing for the YMCA with all your effort and **representing Christ** well through your attitude and actions brings Him glory.

God created you in a way that **brings Him glory** like no one else can. The same is true for **all** God's children. He's **delighted** when His children use the gifts He's given them to honor Him.

Kristin

• •

FROM GOD:

- ♥ "As each has received a gift, use it to serve one another, as good stewards of God's varied grace" (1 Peter 4:10 ESV).
- ♥ "You have given him dominion over the works of your hands; you have put all things under his feet" (Psalm 8:6 ESV).

GO AHEAD—ANSWER:

»⟶ What kinds of gifts and talents has God given you?
»⟶ How do you use these gifts to honor God? In the church? Outside of the church?
»⟶ How can you "waste" a gift?

FROM KRISTIN:

Always keep God the main focus of your heart, and be careful not to make your talent or ambitions your idol.

FROM SUSIE:

God has blessed you with special gifts. What you do with them, and how you use them, is your gift back to Him.

Read books about missions. Give to the missions fund in your local church. Do everything you can to go on a mission trip. It's life changing to give yourself away.

Each summer I (Susie) take a few hundred students (and about seventy-five adults) on a **two-week** international mission trip. We've been to Bolivia, Costa Rica, **Brazil**, Venezuela, Peru, Panama, Ecuador, and Guatemala multiple times. Each trip is a **life-changing** experience. That's why we call it "Never the Same" missions.

Fifteen-year-old Cara's life will **never be the same** after she scooped up a fourteen-month-old baby girl from the dump in Brazil and held her naked little body in her arms. "What are these **red** marks on her bottom?" Cara asked the baby's mom.

"Those are rat bites. We can't keep them away at night when we're in the dump."

Cara **decided** right then to begin supporting a mission outreach program near the dump so she could make sure the little girl had diapers to wear and food to eat.

Charlie was seventeen when he **prayed** for a ninety-year-old Guatemalan man to accept Christ. He placed his **hands** on the man's **ears** as he prayed because the man was **deaf**. With the faith of a spiritually on-fire teenager, Charlie prayed for salvation *and* for healing. Imagine his **delight** when—after he finished the prayer—the man looked at Charlie and exclaimed, "I've been deaf for forty years—since I was fifty! But I **heard** every word of your prayer, and I've accepted Christ as my Savior! He not only forgave my sins, He has healed me!"

Think sixteen-year-old Jessica will ever be the same? She saw God **multiply** water in the slums of Lima, Peru, so she could finish shampooing children's hair, who had never experienced a shampoo in their lives. With only one-half inch of water left in the **basin**, Jessica simply continued to **soap up** the children and rinse their heads as she had promised. Only when she was finished with the last of the ten kids in line did she dare peek down inside the basin. . .to find still one-half inch of water left!

What's the **big deal** about a mission trip? God has made it clear that we're to go into the whole world and spread His message of salvation. And when we go overseas, we enlarge our **worldview**. We also have an opportunity to get out of our comfort zone and trust God more fully.

Do I have to go overseas? **No.** But I hope you can participate in an overseas mission experience at least once in your lifetime. Many students go on local mission trips, and those are powerful, too. But at least once *try* to go **overseas**.

But the fact is, you really don't even have to leave your hometown to be involved in missions. You can support foreign missions by **giving** financially to your own church's missions program. You can also support missions by **praying** faithfully for missionaries. Ask your pastor for a list.

You can also **read books** about missionaries. One book I think everyone ought to read is *The Heavenly Man: The Remarkable True Story of Chinese Christian Brother Yun.* It tells the amazing story of his work with the underground church in China and the persecution he suffered.

Brother Yun is still alive today and serving God with all he has, but he's now living in another country for protection. **Read his story**, and begin praying for persecuted Christians.

If your church offers a mission trip, **pray** about participating. If you don't know of a mission trip being offered, pray about coming with me. You can download the information at: www.neverthesamemissions.org. Your faith will be **stretched**. Your relationship with Christ will take on more meaning. You'll **gain confidence** after praying with someone and leading him or her to Christ. And I promise. . .you will **never be the same!**

Susie

• •

FROM GOD:

❤ "Then Jesus came to them and said, 'All authority in heaven and on earth has been given to me. Therefore go and make disciples of all nations, baptizing them in the name of the Father and of the Son and of the Holy Spirit, and teaching them to obey everything I have commanded you" (Matthew 28:18–20 NIV).

❤ "Preach the word; be prepared in season and out of season" (2 Timothy 4:2 NIV).

GO AHEAD—ANSWER:

»—→ Have you told another person about Christ? If not, what's stopping you? If you have, what was the person's response?

»—→ List some things that make it hard for you to share your faith with others.

»⟶ What can you do to become more comfortable in sharing your faith? Practice more? Grow closer to Christ? Learn more scripture?

FROM SUSIE:

Once you allow God to work through you to lead someone to Him, you'll know that nothing is impossible!

10.

Learn to be a good steward of your money. Try not to get into debt.

The world is out to get you. **Seriously.** That's why the apostle Peter told us to live on the spiritual defense—to keep up our spiritual **guard**. But instead of taking my word for it, read it yourself: "Be careful—watch out for attacks from Satan, your great enemy. He prowls around like a hungry, roaring lion, looking for some victim to tear apart. **Stand firm** when he attacks" (1 Peter 5:8–9 TLB).

Did you catch the **action verbs** in the above scripture? "Be careful!" "Watch out!" We can't be careful, and we can't watch out while sleeping. **We must be alert.**

Satan is causing havoc in the world at every level. And one of the biggest reasons families fall apart is over the issue of **money**. Too many of us aren't **being careful** or **watching out** when it comes to finances.

Here's the deal: if Satan can tempt you into spending like crazy, he has a foothold in your life. *What's a foothold?* Glad you asked. It's like allowing the enemy to **grab** your foot. Someone who's holding your foot doesn't have control of your whole life, but he can **slow you down** and easily trip you. You can still walk, but it gets difficult after a while.

Big businesses are onto you. They've done the research. They know that students your age are some of their top consumers. That's why they're making it possible for you to get **credit cards** at a younger age now. They know if you'll stack up credit with their bank, they can **control** you.

Finances are an area of your life in which it's okay to be a little paranoid. In other words, go ahead and **refuse to spend** as much as your friends. Resist the latest gadget. Say **no** to buying something, even if you can afford it.

My dad taught me a wise principle years ago. He said, "If you'll always **tithe** 10 percent and **save** 10 percent, you'll be okay financially."

He's ninety now, and he's still saving and tithing. I'm **glad** I learned that lesson when I was young. Make **this** part of your lifestyle: God gets the **first 10 percent** of anything you earn. Then stash another 10 percent in the **bank**. Pay your bills and live on what's left. *But that's hardly anything,* you're probably thinking. It will work. I promise. **Just try it!** It's one of the wisest decisions you'll ever make!

An area in which you *can* spend more **freely** is with the things of the Lord. Be generous in your **giving**. Help send a child to church **camp**. Donate to someone who's earning money for a mission trip.

But don't needlessly go into debt. You may *have* to go into debt to get through college, and **that's okay**. A degree is worth the debt. You'll pay that off eventually. But don't spend just to spend. Know that money is valuable, and **God expects** you to make wise decisions with the money He entrusts to you.

Susie

. . . .

FROM GOD:

- ♥ "Let no debt remain outstanding. . ." (Romans 13:8 NIV).
- ♥ "One gives freely, yet grows all the richer; another withholds what he should give, and only suffers want" (Proverbs 11:24 ESV).

GO AHEAD—ANSWER:

- »→ Make a list of all the financial debts you have. What specific course of action can you take to reduce your debt in the next six months?
- »→ What are some things you could do relating to ministry if you weren't in debt?
- »→ Are you consistently tithing 10 percent of all you earn? If not, ask God to help you obey Him with your finances and begin tithing.

FROM SUSIE:

I've learned we can never outgive the Lord! If we'll obey Him and tithe 10 percent, He'll take care of the rest.

FROM KRISTIN:

It's much harder to crawl out of debt than it is to stay out of it in the first place. Ask someone to help you learn to budget if you're not naturally good with that sort of thing.

11.
Wear crazy socks.

I'm in love with **socks.**

Actually, I love colorful socks, **wild watches**, and really wacko shoes that are flat because I can't wear heels. I'm afraid I'll fall. Okay, I'm not afraid I'll fall, but it's just **too much** to think about. Flats are more comfy.

I have five sock drawers. **Five sock drawers.**

Five sock drawers **jammed** with socks. Very colorful socks. Creative socks. **Holiday** socks. Dress socks. Casual socks. Athletic socks. And I love **every** pair. Maybe I get a little carried away, but **crazy socks** make me feel good!

When I pull on a pair of wacko, fun, colorful socks that do or don't go with whatever I'm wearing, **I feel good.** My socks get my creative juices going. I think better and faster. I feel **confident** because I know no one else is wearing what I have on! (**No one else has the guts.** Ha!)

And my **feet** are happy. When my feet are happy, my face smiles. When my face smiles, I greet people. When I greet people, they feel comfortable talking to me. When they talk to me, **I talk back.** We get a conversation going. I find out **his** name: Wendell. I tell him **my** name (Taylor Swift). He doesn't really believe me, but he's polite and pretends he does. **He asks me** about my latest album, and I dance for a moment—making sure my creative socks are showing—and tell him I think it's my **best** work. Then he wants to know about what it's like to live on a tour bus for months at a time. I explain that **I'm used to it** and the gentle roll of the bus actually helps me sleep and when I'm at home in my own bed it's kind of hard to sleep without the rumbling so I'm considering installing a **motor** underneath the headboard. He says he thinks that would give him a **headache**, and I explain that's simply the difference between us creative sock-wearing **stars** and normal people. He looks a bit hurt, so I smile and compliment his pocket watch—I'm assuming it's a pocket watch. I see the little chain coming out of his pocket and attached to his belt. I guess it could be connected to a bell of some sort. But no, it's a **pocket watch** because he pulls it out, nods, and tells me it once belonged to his great-grand-father. I let him know that I love **watches** but can't figure out what good a watch is that you have to keep pulling out of your pocket every time you wanna know what time it is and he says, "That's simply the difference between us creative pocket-watch wearers and you **normal** people." Without thinking, I blurt out, "I am **not** normal!" He smiles. And I scream, "I mean, I am **too** normal. I mean. . .I have five sock drawers at home." Wendell turns and walks away, and I can't help but notice that he's wearing orange socks. "Wendell!" I half-scream, half-gasp. But he can't hear me now. Traffic has picked up, and it's starting to rain. I sigh. Oh, Wendell. How many sock drawers do **you** have?

Susie

• •

FROM GOD:

💗 "Live creatively, friends" (Galatians 6:1 MSG).

💗 "Make a careful exploration of who you are and the work you have been given, and then sink yourself into that. Don't be impressed with yourself. Don't compare yourself with others. Each of you must take responsibility for doing the creative best you can with your own life" (Galatians 6:4–5 MSG).

GO AHEAD—ANSWER:

»→ Describe something fun and eccentric you have that makes you feel good.

»→ Think of an eccentric gift you can give someone who will truly appreciate the creativity behind it.

»→ Learn to enjoy the eccentricities of others.

FROM SUSIE:

I found out it would cost too much to install a motor underneath my headboard, so I settled for a little fan on my nightstand.

FROM KRISTIN:

There's no better feeling in the world than taking off your socks at the end of a long day.

12.

Find your security, identity, and confidence in Christ, not people.

Do the **approval**, attention, and praise of others make you feel important? One of the easiest traps to fall into is looking to others to give you **value**. The problem with putting your security, **identity**, and confidence in people is that eventually they'll mishandle it. We're all human, so it's only a matter of time before someone gets let down.

It's easy to **feel great** when Mom and Dad brag about your good grades, the coaches love you 'cause you're the fastest runner on the track team, and your friends want to hang out with you all the time.

But **what if** your grades slip? **What if** you get injured, or someone else joins your sports team who's much better? **What if** your friends decide not to hang out with you anymore? Do you still feel loved, treasured, and important?

You are!

"See what kind of love the Father has given to us, that we should be called children of God; and so we are" (1 John 3:1 ESV).

You're a **daughter of God**. The same God who put every star in the sky, every fish in the sea, and knows the number of hairs on every single human head calls *you* **His child**. Take a second and **think** about that.

No, really. **Think about it!**

You're **not** more important if you're extra talented at sports or music. You aren't worth less because you don't have the proportions of a supermodel. God **delights** as much in you when you're asleep as He does when you're awake and using your brains. People look at your appearance or accomplishments to give you value, but **God** looks at the **heart**.

And guess what—if your heart is filled with Jesus, you're treasured solely because you're a **daughter of the King**.

"And if children, then heirs—heirs of God and fellow heirs with Christ" (Romans 8:17 ESV).

If you've put your faith in Jesus, then you're a princess, an **heir** to the throne of grace. Remember all those movies where a character finds out she's a princess? It's kind of like that, except this is real life!

God has prepared a special place in His kingdom. It's waiting for you right now. (Don't use that as an excuse to be reckless. It'll still be there if you live a nice, long life.)

Here's the **difficult part**. We have to wait until the next life for our inheritance. In fact, the **next part** of Romans 8:17 tells us that if we are to share in Christ's glory, we must share in His suffering.

Uh-oh. What does *that* mean?

It means that life won't always be easy. You won't always be treated like a princess. You'll fail, make mistakes, get teased, and go through trials. But **none** of those things can ever take away your **value** or your status as **God's daughter** or your place in the kingdom of heaven.

Think of your self-worth as money. Would you put it in a bank with a reputation for robberies? Of course not!

If you place your **worth** in God, He'll protect it. God **promises** never to leave or forsake us. He promises to **walk** alongside us in trials. God's place in His kingdom is **waiting** for you in heaven. And *that* you can count on. **Always!**

Kristin

● ●

FROM GOD:

- 💜 "And if children, then heirs; heirs of God, and joint-heirs with Christ; if so be that we suffer with him, that we may be also glorified with him" (Romans 8:17 ASV).
- 💜 "According to his great mercy, he has caused us to be born again to a living hope through the resurrection of Jesus Christ from the dead, to an inheritance that is imperishable, undefiled, and unfading, kept in heaven for you" (1 Peter 1:3–4 ESV).

GO AHEAD—ANSWER:

- »→ Have you ever thought about how much God loves you through all circumstances? I mean *really* thought about it?
- »→ Does understanding how much God values you change the way you live your life? How?
- »→ Describe some of the ways that God shows His love for you.

FROM KRISTIN:

Write the above verses on index cards and keep them with you. Better yet—memorize them!

13.
Hang around with people outside your peer group.

You can learn a lot from adults, and younger kids can learn a lot from you.

I can already hear you. "Seriously? What can I **learn** from adults?"

A lot—if they're from your **church**. Most of the adults there know all the words to the old **hymns**, and one of these days some radio deejay is going to ask a trivia question like, "What's the next line of this old hymn from 'The Old Rugged Cross'?"

On a hill far away stood an old rugged cross,
The emblem of suffering and shame.

And you're going to realize that you've never even heard the song—let alone know it—and the prize will be a brand-new **BMW** with all the extras because a Christian guy who has his own automobile dealership is giving it away to the local Christian radio station to help him on taxes and **weird stuff** like that and you're desperate for a car because you're sick of riding your **unicycle** everywhere and bumming rides off everyone else and you'd feel really important driving a brand-new **Beemer** and picking up your friends and driving them to school and to Sonic during **Happy Hour** for a half-priced Blue Coconut Slush and you know you'll never be able to save enough money to **buy your own** Beemer because you're just not that organized and your part-time job at the Shoe Barn only pays minimum wage and you can only work **three hours** a day because of school, oboe lessons, youth group, and chores at home, and if you've been hanging out with Mr. Thompson who's **retired** but still serves as the church janitor or with Mrs. Wingate who **bakes bread** for all the visitors you'll feel comfortable getting the answer and calling in the next line to the radio deejay:

And I love that old cross where the dearest and best
For a world of lost sinners was slain.

And the deejay will be so **surprised** that you have the correct answer so quickly that he'll even throw in a set of new **floor mats**, too, and you'll get the brand-new Beemer and possibly by continuing to hang out with the older people you'll learn how to use proper punctuation and not write run-on sentences.

And for the little kids? How else would you remember how yummy and fun graham crackers and juice boxes are? **So go ahead.** Hang with them. A little. Not too much. Because, you know, crackers and juice will spoil your dinner.

Susie

FROM GOD:

- ❤ "Stand up in the presence of the aged, show respect for the elderly and revere your God. I am the LORD" (Leviticus 19:32 NIV).
- ❤ "At that time Jesus said, 'I praise you, Father, Lord of heaven and earth, because you have hidden these things from the wise and learned, and revealed them to little children' " (Matthew 11:25 NIV).

GO AHEAD—ANSWER:

»—→ What specifically can you do this week to show respect for the elderly?

»—→ What can you do to bless an elderly person this week?

»—→ What can you do to make a child feel important this week?

FROM SUSIE:

Grab some crayons and a coloring book and enjoy the afternoon with a child. Or get a couple of yo-yos and hang out with a younger teen. OR... play a board game with an elderly person.

14.

Take correction that's given in love, but let baseless criticism roll off your back.

Though criticism always hurts, **sometimes** it can be helpful. But gossip, **useless arguments**, mundane talk, shallow conversation, and **unfounded criticism** aren't worth losing sleep over.

But how do you know the difference? Ahhh. This is where **discernment** comes in. If someone says, "The last three times you've given me a ride to the **football** game, you've been late," that's worth thinking about.

Is there a **reason** you're late? If you know you're going to be late, why not **call your friend** and explain why? Are you waiting until the last minute to put gas in the car? Are you not paying attention to the time? Are you too busy to pick her up on time?

Think the situation through, **apologize**, and correct your behavior. Being late will never get you ahead. It *can* get you **fired**, cost you friends, cause you to miss the sale, and give you a bad reputation. **This is helpful criticism.**

But if someone tries to pin any or all of the following on you, let it roll off your back. Pay no attention. **Forget it.** Tune out. But make sure you're always on time. That really **is** important!

—You **skate** funny.

—The hair on your arm is too thick.

—You use the wrong kind of toothpaste.

—You smile too much.

—You use the wrong kind of soap.

—You can't make **popcorn** that tastes as good as the theater's. (So what? No one can.)

—You're too conservative.

—The carpet in your house is ugly.

— Your hair would look much better if it were purple and dipped in glitter. **Or hot fudge.**

—Your knee is wobbly.

—Your voice stinks. (How can a voice smell bad? That doesn't even make sense.)

—You fold your **T-shirts** incorrectly.

—How come you never eat brussels sprouts? (Uhhhh, because they're gross.)

—Your **second toe** is longer than your big toe.

—Your cell phone ring is stupid.

—Your skin looks **yellow**. (If it really does, you need to see a doctor. If it really doesn't, respond with, "You're color-blind.")

—You're color-blind. (Good time to say, "Your **skin** looks yellow.")

—How come you're never on time? (Okay, we've already talked about this!)

Susie

• •

FROM GOD:

♥ "A perverse person stirs up conflict, and a gossip separates close friends" (Proverbs 16:28 NIV).

♥ "Stay away from foolish, useless talk, because that will lead people further away from God" (2 Timothy 2:16 NCV).

GO AHEAD—ANSWER:

»→ The next time someone gossips to you or shares unfair criticism, what can you say or do to end the conversation?

»→ Will you ask God to help you speak words of encouragement to others instead of criticism?

»→ Think of three genuine compliments you can hand out today, and do it.

FROM SUSIE:

It's a proven fact: by age four, children around the world—in all languages—all know one universal phrase: "Nyah, nyah, nyah, nyah, nyah." Please don't carry this into your adult vocabulary. You won't get the job.

15.
Raise a chicken.

You might be asking yourself **why** an advice book for teens is suggesting you raise a chicken. **What** does that have to do with growing up?

In reality, raising a chicken is **not** essential to crossing the bridge to adulthood. It just makes the **journey** a little more exciting.

Before getting a chicken you'll have to do two things. First, you'll have to check with your **parents**. Second, you'll have to check with your **residential area** to see if your neighborhood allows animals, like chickens.

If both are a yes, call some area feed stores and ask when they get their spring chicks (it's often around March or April). A **baby chick** usually costs less than a chicken sandwich. Weird, huh?

Chickens are both **funny** to watch and **practical** to have around. Want hours of entertainment? Watch chickens interact. My sister and I once threw a wildflower into our chicken coop. One chicken grabbed it while the other nine got instantly jealous and chased it around the coop in circles trying to grab the flower from its mouth.

If you need some **practical** reasons, I've taken the liberty of creating a comprehensive list of why every girl should own at least *one* **chicken** in her lifetime:

- Chickens eat bugs and help keep your yard pest-free.
- Their poop makes great fertilizer for your lawn. (Can I say *poop* in here? Huh?) [Note to reader: If the word *poop* is still here when you're reading this book, I guess it's okay. If it's NOT in here and there's just a blank space, feel free to write the word *poop* in the space provided.]
- They lay tasty, nutritious eggs. When was the last time your dog or cat created something you could eat? (If you answer something other than "never" to that question, please, please, *please* e-mail us. That's a story for our next book!)
- You'll feel like you're on *Little House on the Prairie*.
- You have a greater chance of finally solving the mystery of why the chicken crossed the road.

Kristin

FROM GOD:

❤ "I know all the birds of the hills, and all that moves in the field is mine" (Psalm 50:11 ESV).

❤ "Look at the birds of the air: they neither sow nor reap nor gather into barns, and yet your heavenly Father feeds them. Are you not of more value than they?" (Matthew 6:26 ESV).

GO AHEAD—ANSWER:

»—→ Do you own a pet? What does taking care of something dependent on you teach you about how God takes care of us?

»—→ Does knowing that God takes care of the smallest creatures make you trust Him more to supply your needs? Why or why not?

»—→ Describe some ways that you could you be a "good steward" of an abundance of farm-fresh eggs?

FROM KRISTIN:

Okay—I'm going to answer the last question for you. Fresh eggs are great for reaching out to people. Offer to have them come over with an empty egg carton to pick them out, and take a few minutes to get to know them!

FROM SUSIE:

I just wanted to see if I could say poop in here, too.

16.

Be trustworthy. Don't take your promises lightly, and keep your word when you give it.

This is important because it affects your **character** and your **reputation**. Let's chat about character first. Your character is built from distinguishable **traits** that individually define **you**. Your character is what can make you **stand** head and shoulders above everyone else; it's what makes you trustworthy. Good character is defined by values such as honesty, loyalty, **dependability**, and morality.

Your reputation will **always** align with your character. Your character is who you are—what defines you. And your reputation is everyone's knowledge of your character.

So if you have a habit of lying, your **character** won't reflect trustworthiness and you'll have a reputation of being dishonest. Again, your character and your reputation **always** align. If you're dependable, you'll have the reputation of being someone people can **count** on.

So don't give your word lightly. When you commit to something—whether it's huge (like building an imitation of the Taj Mahal for history class) or small (such as saying you'll bring paper cups to the BBQ Friday evening), think it through *before* you make the commitment.

You may *think* it's **no big deal** to say you'll bring paper cups to Friday evening's event, but when you forget and show up at the party to see your friends having to share the host's **toothpaste** cup to drink lemonade, you'll be totally embarrassed. (And that's why it's good to make a list of important stuff. See Tip #54!)

People want friends they can count on. Because Christ is our role model, let's take a quick peek at His life. When He said something, He meant it. When He committed, He did it. **He always kept His word.** And thousands of years later, **He's still keeping His word.** We know we can trust Him. We enjoy the fact that He's dependable.

Imagine **yesterday** you prayed, "Jesus, I really need Your help tomorrow with my job interview. I need You to calm my nerves and to help me answer the questions I'll be asked with confidence."

Today you're walking into the interview and praying, "Okay, Lord. It's time. Please calm me down. Help me to do great with this."

How would you feel if He answered, "Uh, yeah. **About that.** I totally spaced it. I'm helping someone find a parking space at Wal-Mart right now. You're on your own with this one."

Christ keeps His word, and as His follower, He expects you to do the same. **Don't be wishy-washy.** Determine to develop a strong reputation of being trustworthy and dependable. When you tell someone you'll do something, do it—even if you have to rearrange your schedule. . .and even if it costs you!

If you're not sure you can follow through, simply don't commit. **Never say yes unless you're sure!**

Susie

• •

FROM GOD:

♥ "Let your yes be YES. Let your no be NO" (Matthew 5:37 NLV).
♥ "It is better not to make a vow than to make one and not fulfill it" (Ecclesiastes 5:5 NIV).

GO AHEAD—ANSWER:

»—→ Identify a time in your life you overcommitted yourself. What was the outcome? What were the consequences? What did you learn?
»—→ How do you respond when a friend says she'll do something but doesn't follow through?
»—→ How can you develop a reputation of keeping your word?

FROM SUSIE:

I want friends to know they can count on me. If I have to stay up late or skip something I wanted to do in order to keep my word, I'll do it.

17.

Take an apologetics course.

Has anyone ever told you the Bible can't be backed up **scientifically** or histori-cally? That **God** doesn't exist? That humans **made Him up** because we needed something to make us feel meaningful?

Could you answer them?

Being able to give a defense of your faith is called **apologetics**. (And by the way, we actually have more historic proof that the Bible is true than we have proof that Shakespeare wrote *Romeo and Juliet*.) Atheists and other nonbelievers are constantly hurling **arguments** against the existence of God or the deity of Jesus Christ. **At first glance** some of these arguments sound convincing. Once you look closer, though, **truth** begins shining through.

Here are a few arguments you may come up against:

- There's **no** absolute truth.

Is that absolutely true?

- You can't **see, touch, taste, or feel** God; therefore, He must not exist.

*You can't **see, touch, taste, or feel** the brain of someone who tells you that. **Does that mean it doesn't exist?** You **know** it exists by outside evidence! If a person is forming orderly ideas, they must have a brain. If the entire universe bears the mark of incredible order, something intelligent **must** be behind it.*

- Jesus **never** rose from the grave. The apostles made that up so they could create their own religion.

*Did you know the **first** people in the biblical account to run into **Jesus** after He rose were **women**? This may not mean much today, but in biblical times the testimony of a woman meant **nothing**. No one would believe what a woman said. If you were going to **make up** a religion, wouldn't you **make sure** to have the witness of someone whose story could be used in court? You'd make sure a **man** was the first to see Jesus. **But that's not what the Bible does.** It accounts truth, even if it goes against what was politically correct at the time.*

Those are just **a few of many** arguments you'll hear during your lifetime, and as a believer you need to know **why** you believe **what** you believe. Read some great books on apologetics. Check out these authors: Josh McDowell, Alex McFar-land, Lee Strobel. . . . They've all written some fantastic books on apologetics.

Also, try to find out if any churches near you offer apologetics classes or seminars. No? Then search your local Christian bookstore or go online for some apologetics curriculum.

Arguments and knowledge won't change a hardened heart. Only the Holy Spirit can do that. God may use your ready defense, though, to stir that person's heart to their sin and need for a Savior.

Knowing apologetics will not only make you a more effective witness, it will **strengthen** your own faith as you learn more than ever that Christianity is **the Ultimate Truth**.

Kristin

• •

FROM GOD:

❤ "But in your hearts honor Christ the Lord as holy, always being prepared to make a defense to anyone who asks you for a reason for the hope that is in you; yet do it with gentleness and respect" (1 Peter 3:15 ESV).

❤ "We destroy arguments and every lofty opinion raised against the knowledge of God, and take every thought captive to obey Christ" (2 Corinthians 10:5 ESV).

GO AHEAD—ANSWER:

»→ Has anyone ever brought arguments to you against Christianity? Were you able to answer? What did you say?

»→ Have you ever had doubts about the truth of the Bible? How did you reconcile these doubts? Did you search for answers?

»→ Why do you think God tells us to be prepared to make a defense?

FROM KRISTIN:

Apologetics isn't about "winning" the debate, it's about pointing people to the saving grace of Jesus Christ. It's important to be equipped with answers for why you believe what you believe, but it's more important to demonstrate the love of Christ. So after you gently point out the errors in someone's thinking, bake them cookies.

18.
Be kind with your words.

You have the ability to **make** or **break** someone's day with your words. Choose **words** that will uplift, encourage, and affirm. There are three exciting things about using your words in a positive way.

1. *You're being Christ-like.* During His time on earth, Christ loved **encouraging** those around Him. As we read His words, we often hear Him saying, "Don't be afraid." "**I love you.**" "I call you My friends." "I'll never leave you."

And in the **Old Testament**, we often hear Father God also using His words to uplift His children: "I have plans to **prosper** you." "I have chosen you." "I call you by name; **you're Mine.**" So anytime you make the choice to use your words to uplift someone, you're doing what God wants you to do!

2. *You'll become a people magnet.* It's a fact: we love being around those who make us **feel good**. We're naturally attracted to people who are encouragers. After you've left someone who has affirmed you, you usually can't wait to see her again, simply because you've been uplifted by her words. **It's a ministry.** And it's a ministry you can easily develop!

3. *It's easy.* You don't have to be a rocket scientist to figure out which words will uplift and affirm and which words will discourage and destroy. In fact, **test yourself** right now. Circle the phrases that would encourage you, and mark through those that would discourage you.

- "Wow. Where have you been shopping? The garbage dump?"
- "I never noticed how beautiful your handwriting is! Your penmanship is so good, it could be a font."
- "That color looks great on you."
- "Uh, you got a little somethin' somethin' coming out on your nose. What *is* that—a *double* zit?"
- "Great to see you!"

Make a conscious choice right now to be **kind** with your words! You'll make God **proud,** and you'll soon notice that people will want to start hanging around you. Go ahead—make someone's day!

Susie

FROM GOD:

- ♥ "Gracious words are a honeycomb, sweet to the soul and healing to the bones" (Proverbs 16:24 NIV).
- ♥ "Do not let any unwholesome talk come out of your mouths, but only what is helpful for building others up according to their needs, that it may benefit those who listen" (Ephesians 4:29 NIV).

GO AHEAD—ANSWER:

- »—→ What specifically do you need to do in order to begin using words that will uplift others? Do you need a major overhaul, a slight change, or accountability?
- »—→ Think of three people whom you can verbally encourage today, and do it.
- »—→ Ask God to transform your conversations so they please and glorify Him.

FROM SUSIE:

No good word is ever wasted. And kind words aren't forgotten. I still remember specific words of encouragement from youth leaders, teachers, my parents, and friends—even though spoken years ago—that have made a positive difference in my life!

19.
Find the humor in things.

Did you spend an **hour** on your hair only to walk through pouring rain as you entered the school building? So now you're looking like a wet poodle? It's **inconvenient**, but also a little **hilarious**. It's even more hilarious when you look around and see that it happened to everyone else! Why complain about the rain when you can laugh about the results?

God ordained **humor and laughter**. If you don't believe me, just look at pictures of a duck-billed platypus, or go to the zoo and watch a giraffe pick its nose with its tongue.

One of the best things about being a Christian is that our hope is secure. We know that no matter what happens **here**, we get to spend eternity in **paradise** with the God of the universe. This means we're free to **laugh** about the silly things in life. Not everything has to be taken so seriously!

The Bible tells us that there's "a time to weep, and a time to laugh; a time to mourn, and a time to dance" (Ecclesiastes 3:4 ESV).

There are certain times when laughter is **not** appropriate—such as the moment your friend is sharing her struggles, or you're in class and the teacher's trying to lecture. However, if you get teased because you accidentally put on two clashing socks, don't be embarrassed. **Laugh!** Besides, if you wear those socks confidently, you could start the next fashion trend!

Kristin

• •

FROM GOD:

❤ "He will yet fill your mouth with laughter, and your lips with shouting" (Job 8:21 ESV).

❤ "A joyful heart is good medicine, but a crushed spirit dries up the bones" (Proverbs 17:22 ESV).

GO AHEAD—ANSWER:

»→ What are three things that make you laugh out loud?

»→ Are you easily offended when people tease you? Or can you laugh with them?

>>→ Why do you think God wants us to laugh and be joyful?

FROM KRISTIN:

Find ways to have fun and laugh with your family and friends. Watch some clean stand-up comedy, read a silly story, or play a fun game like Telephone Pictionary or charades.

20.
You don't need 750 self-portraits on Facebook (or anywhere else).

May I be **honest** with you? Are you sure? The truth might **sting** a little.

The constant need to take and post self-portraits on your social media site reveals you may have some insecurity, **vanity**, and self-absorption issues.

Facebook and other social media are wonderful tools. We can keep in touch with friends, encourage one another, and **share our lives** in a way that was impossible in the dark ages of the '90s. However, they also have the power to reveal our **sinful nature**.

The freedom to say and post whatever you want, whenever you want, shows your **true** colors. It's not about the actual posting; it's about where your heart is and why.

Ask yourself:

- *What's my motivation for posting forty-seven pictures of myself in a row?*
- *Do the comments and "likes" give me a self-esteem boost?*
- *If no one responds to my post, do I feel **rejected** and hurt?*
- *Who am I hoping will notice? **Guys?***
- *Do I want to make girls **jealous** of how I look?*

The Bible challenges us to think of ourselves **less**. Does spending an hour taking and posting pictures of yourself online glorify God? The Bible calls this **vanity**, and it displeases God.

Your friends don't need to see sixty pictures of you in the fitting-room mirror holding your camera phone. **Instead**, take some friends, siblings, or your mom with you shopping and focus on **spending quality time** with people face-to-face. Don't make the day about putting pictures of yourself on Facebook.

If you *must* have a self-portrait up, one is *really* all you need, with a couple of **exceptions:**

Exception #1: If you're in a really **exciting** location, and there's absolutely no one around to take your picture, and you want proof you were there, a self-portrait is okay.

Exception #2: If you're with a friend being goofy, self-portraits can be fun. You don't, however, need to post every single picture on Facebook. One is enough.

Still, it's best to just ask someone to take your picture! I bet they'll say yes, and you'll get more of the exciting background in the shot. Plus, it's a great way to meet new people!

Kristin

• •

FROM GOD:

💜 "Do nothing from selfish ambition or conceit, but in humility count others more significant than yourselves. Let each of you look not only to his own interests, but also to the interests of others" (Philippians 2:3–4 ESV).

💜 "Turn my eyes from looking at worthless things; and give me life in your ways" (Psalm 119:37 ESV).

GO AHEAD—ANSWER:

»—→ Are you guilty of posting hundreds of self-portraits? Think about the underlying heart issue. Why do you want people looking at you?

»—→ What are some ways you can honor God with your social media use?

»—→ Do you find social media sucking you in constantly? Think about setting some boundaries to keep it from consuming all your time and attention.

FROM KRISTIN:

Ask God to fulfill your longing to be noticed, approved, and validated. Don't put that in the hands of the "like" button.

21.

Pray for persecuted Christians. A lot.

Imagine: It's Sunday morning, and you're in church. The worship leader and band strike up your favorite praise song. You join in with the congregation around you when **suddenly** the drummer stops. Something's wrong with the words on the **screen**. Or maybe it's the screen itself. You squint. There's a hole in the screen!

The worship leader has stopped. The fast-paced rhythm of gunfire quickly replaces the rhythm of music. This place of praise has become a place of panic. Militants have entered the sanctuary and have opened fire.

Nineteen members of your church have already been shot. Others are running, falling, searching for safety. There **is** none. Several people you know are led away with guns pointed at their heads. After another round of open fire sprays the congregation, the militants leave, celebrating their victory.

It's Wednesday evening, and only ten minutes after youth group has started, **police** burst in and drag you, your classmates, and your leader to the police station for questioning. They want to know what you're doing and whether you're **breaking the law**.

A pastor sits in prison, awaiting execution. His crime? **Challenging** religious teachings in his children's school.

Do these sound made-up?

You can stop imagining now.

The pretend game is over.

At least for you.

But unfortunately, these are real scenarios for many Christians living around the globe.

For some people, **living** for Christ means **dying** for Him. It means losing everything and facing a life of **oppression**.

It's easy to take our religious freedoms for granted. We can meet at Starbucks for Bible study, pray at flagpoles, and invite our friends to church.

"First of all, then, I urge that supplications, prayers, intercessions, and thanksgivings be made for all people, for kings and all who are in high positions, that we may lead a peaceful and quiet life, godly and dignified in every way" (1 Timothy 2:1–2 ESV).

Don't feel guilty about being able to worship freely, but **don't** take these gifts for granted. Thank God for your freedoms, and **pray** that the leaders of our country let us keep **worshiping in peace**. Study your Bible, pray, and consistently worship with other believers.

Also, spend time praying for those living in **persecuted** countries. Need a place to start? Ask God to give your spiritual brothers and sisters **joy**, peace, **steadfastness**, justice, and **safety**. Pray that families can stay together, pray for provision, and **pray for the gospel to spread** despite oppression.

Also, pray for those who are persecuting the Christians. Pray that they, too, will come to know the **great love of Jesus**. Paul persecuted Christians before God revealed Himself to him and made him one of the greatest evangelists in history.

Other things you can do? Sign petitions and **write letters** to Christians imprisoned around the globe. Give money to organizations that supply Bibles and other supplies to persecuted nations.

Kristin

. . . .

FROM GOD:

♥ "Remember those who are in prison, as though in prison with them, and those who are mistreated, since you also are in the body" (Hebrews 13:3 ESV).

♥ "So Peter was kept in prison, but earnest prayer for him was made to God by the church" (Acts 12:5 ESV).

GO AHEAD—ANSWER:

»—→ Share a time when you've been teased for your faith. Do you know others who have been mocked as well?

»—→ Think of a few things you can do with your church or youth group to help support Christians in persecuted countries. What did you come up with?

»—→ Have you thanked God today for your religious freedoms? If not, take a minute and do that now.

FROM KRISTIN:

If you'd like to find specific needs of those being persecuted around the world, a good starting point is Voice of the Martyrs at www.persecution.com.

FROM SUSIE:

This is so serious! Please pray for Christians who are being persecuted. Kristin and I both feel very strongly about this need.

Determine to be friendly to everyone—regardless of looks, color of skin, class, or popularity. This **prevents** you from taking sides, keeps you away from drama, and helps against being bullied.

Even God warns against **senseless** drama: "Don't have anything to do with foolish and stupid arguments, because you know they produce quarrels" (2 Timothy 2:23 NIV).

It seems most major drama revolves around relationships:

- She was my best friend, but suddenly she likes Hannah more than me.
- She knows I'm crushing on Evan, but she went out with him anyway!
- I told her not to tell anyone. Now the whole school knows!
- I didn't know how to tell her that she's overbearing, so I just stopped being her friend.

Avoiding relationship drama requires thinking ~~twice, four times, overtime,~~ **a lot** about what you say before you say it. This is tough. In fact, it's reallyreallyreally tough!

If you seriously don't want **anyone** to know that you're crushing on Brandon, **don't tell** anyone! Even though Rachel is your best friend and you feel you have to tell her or you'll **explode**, you're still taking a risk. And if she *does* let it slip, **don't blame her.** You didn't have to tell her. Talk with your mom, or keep a journal.

When Conner asks you to sit with him at the basketball game, and you know Tiffany has a crush on him, **be careful.** If convenient, grab Tiffany and a couple of other gal pals and guide everyone to sit with Conner.

And when your **best friend** starts hanging out with someone else and you're suddenly feeling left out? Ask **both** of them to go to the movies, come to your house, hit the mall. If your best friend seems resistant, give her some space. Maybe you're too possessive or she just needs to spread her wings a little. Give her that **freedom**. Keep being **nice** to her, but don't try to **control** the situation.

Strive to be everyone's biggest **cheerleader** instead of someone who creates division, tension, and arguments.

Is it ever okay to get involved in drama? **Sure.** If there's a moral issue at stake, take a stand. If someone's being bullied, put a stop to it. Take the under-dog's side. **Never** support bullying, and never stand by simply doing nothing. Take sides!

And if you're still yearning for some drama? Enroll for it. As in drama class. The school play. Go ahead. Audition. *Bye Bye Birdie*, *Annie Get Your Gun*, *You're a Good Man, Charlie Brown*, *Oklahoma!*, *The Music Man*, *Our Town*. That's good drama!

Susie

• •

FROM GOD:

♥ "Would they argue with useless words, with speeches that have no value?" (Job 15:3 NIV).

♥ "Get rid of all bitterness, rage, anger, harsh words, and slander, as well as all types of evil behavior" (Ephesians 4:31 NLT).

GO AHEAD—ANSWER:

»→ Some people argue simply to argue. This is a sign of insecurity. What can you do to avoid these kinds of arguments?

»→ What kinds of relationship drama tempt you to use harsh words? What would be a better way of handling the situation?

»→ What specifically can you do to help prevent bullying?

FROM SUSIE:

As a former high school drama teacher, I encourage you to save the dramatics for a stage and a paying audience.

FROM KRISTIN:

Some people don't know how to function without drama. I call these people "codependent on drama." Be very careful around these people—they will make any situation about them!

23.
Be fierce about staying pure.

In fact, when it comes to sexual purity, you can take any of these labels as a compliment: prude, straight, freak, narrow, (fill in the blank).

Is sexual **purity** really that big of a deal? It's tough to find a TV sitcom, drama, **reality show**, or movie without watching the characters pair off and sleep together at the end of a **date**. And you probably know students who are into **FWB**, right? (Friends With Benefits: being sexually involved with someone with no strings attached; no relationship; no commitment.)

Sex is everywhere! Commercials advertising a new soft drink with a barely clothed female holding the drink, perfume ads, sports equipment. It doesn't matter what the product is—if a half-naked guy or girl is toting it, statistics prove that it **sells** better.

So why the **big deal** about sexual purity? Again, sex is everywhere!

Okay. Time to bring it home. Yes, sex is **rampant**. So was the bubonic plague. It's also known as the **Black Death** and wiped out 30 to 60 percent of the European population in the fourteenth century. **Just because** something is everywhere doesn't mean it's good.

But **sex** _can_ be good—in the right context—which is **always** marriage. Because **God created sex**, it's His gift to us. And His gift, when opened at the right time, is great. But like opening a Christmas **gift** ahead of time, there are consequences with not waiting.

I know married **couples** who have struggled for decades with sex simply because they fooled around before marriage. After they were married, the **guilt** from messing around sexually was so strong that building a good sex life has been a real struggle.

Be fierce about your purity. **Guard it with your life!** To do this, you'll want to be extremely selective about what you watch on TV and the big screen. You'll also be **careful** about what you read, the music you listen to, and the conversations you're involved in. **Check this out:**

"But among you there must not be even a hint of sexual immorality, or of any kind of impurity, or of greed, because these are improper for God's holy people" (Ephesians 5:3 NIV).

Not even a **hint**.

Not even a hint.

Not **even** a hint.
That's being fierce about your purity!
And your future spouse is definitely worth it.

Susie

• •

FROM GOD:

💙 "That is why I say to run from sex sin. No other sin affects the body as this one does" (1 Corinthians 6:18 TLB).

💙 "Marriage should be honored by all, and the marriage bed kept pure, for God will judge the adulterer and all the sexually immoral" (Hebrews 13:4 NIV).

GO AHEAD–ANSWER:

»⟶ In what ways does sexual sin affect the body that other sin doesn't? For example, how would sinning sexually affect you worse than gossip?

»⟶ Create a strategy that will enable you to run from sexual immorality. This may need to involve accountability.

»⟶ What can you do now to honor your future marriage bed?

FROM SUSIE:

If you've been sexually involved, you can ask God to forgive you. He'd love to give you a new start and help you create clear boundaries for future dating relationships.

FROM KRISTIN:

Don't stay pure just for a husband—stay pure for Jesus because He calls you to it. And remember, God didn't put these standards in place to exasperate us, but because He created us and knows what's best for us!

Wouldn't it be great if holding grudges gave you a six-pack? We'd all look like Olympic athletes! Unfortunately, **grudges** don't help physically. In fact, they can do the **opposite**.

There are some theories that **holding on to anger** can actually cause stomachaches, backaches, and other physical problems.

That's because we weren't created to **shoulder** those kinds of burdens!

"Cast your burden on the Lord, and he will sustain you; he will never permit the righteous to be moved" (Psalm 55:22 esv).

Holding on to anger is a **huge** burden. Let Him take your burdens, grudges, anger, and hurt. Tell God about your struggle to let go, and ask Him to remove it from your heart. You may have to do this **daily** for a while, but eventually you won't think about it anymore!

Grudges don't just rob you physically, they mess you up **spiritually**, too. They rob you of your joy, **peace**, and contentment. You can't be **happy** until the situation is fair. You'll waste time figuring out ways to "get back at her" or "get even."

Don't focus on getting retaliation!

Guess what!

Withholding forgiveness is a way of retaliating.

At its core, unforgiveness shows lack of trust in God. It reveals that we don't think God can or will take care of the situation fairly. Staying angry becomes a **subtle** way of staying in control. Give up this control, and **trust** that God will reveal the sin and change the person in His time. Even if the other person refuses to acknowledge or repent of his fault, **you** still need to forgive. The Bible never says, "Forgive only when someone apologizes to you." It simply says **forgive**.

Forgiveness is for **your good**. It makes you more **like Christ** and increases your **joy**. Forgiveness isn't saying what was done to you is okay. It's simply acknowledging that you're not perfect **either** and you need the same **grace** that forgiveness offers.

We don't forgive because they **deserve** it.

We don't forgive to feel **good** about ourselves.

We forgive because **Christ** forgave us.

Kristin

FROM GOD:

- ❤ "Be kind to one another, tenderhearted, forgiving one another, as God in Christ forgave you" (Ephesians 4:32 ESV).
- ❤ "And whenever you stand praying, forgive, if you have anything against anyone, so that your Father also who is in heaven may forgive your trespasses" (Mark 11:25 ESV).

GO AHEAD—ANSWER:

»⟶ Are you holding on to any grudges right now? What's stopping you from extending forgiveness?

»⟶ Sometimes forgiveness is a daily thing. Who do you need to forgive over and over for the same offense?

»⟶ Have you ever had to ask for forgiveness? How did it feel to apologize? Did the other person extend grace and forgiveness?

FROM KRISTIN:

Forgiveness brings a peace that passes all understanding. You'll know when you've forgiven someone when you can pray for God to bless them—and mean it!

25.
Don't be a social media hypocrite.

We can instantly express our problems, frustrations, anger, need for attention, sadness, arrogance, happiness, and any other feeling under the sun using **social media**.

Facebook, Twitter, Instagram, and Pinterest allow us to tell the world what we're feeling, thinking, and doing. Unfortunately, not everything we feel, think, and do needs to be **announced** to everyone, and it's easy to get hypocritical with our posts.

I see girls claiming to follow Christ posting crude, self-centered, and mean things on their social media. They act one way when you see them in person, and yet their social media shows a completely different—often scarier—side.

How you represent yourself on social media should match how you represent yourself in real life. And **both** of these representations should be God-honoring.

Honoring God with social media doesn't mean you should only post verses, Christian quotes, and links to sermons. It does mean, however, that you **should be aware** of what you post, how it comes across, and be mindful that *anyone* could look at it. In the "real world," offensive, rude, whiny, selfish, or mean social media postings can cost you jobs, friends, opportunities, and **respect**.

Stop fishing for compliments, **swearing**, complaining about people (they may read your posts), **taking "selfies,"** making the "duck face," posting every fourteen seconds, posting pictures of yourself barely clothed, **"subtweeting,"** posting your phone number and asking people to text you to do something, and trying other tactics to get attention. (You know what they are.)

Instead, use your **social media positively**. Share pictures of exciting adventures and places you've been with your family and friends. Post funny, encouraging, thought-provoking, and **uplifting** statuses. Share things that matter. Message your friends, but don't get passive-aggressive. Don't take your anger out in your tweets.

Social media detaches us and easily makes us **shallow**. We can spend lots of time crafting a perfect online image without ever doing anything that will actually contribute to our character and growth as a human. It allows us to portray altered versions of ourselves, showing only what we want people to see and leaving out the parts that wouldn't get as many "likes." We get **jealous** over other people's online lives, forgetting that, like us, they're not sharing the whole story.

Be true, loving, and real. Online and off.

Kristin

• •

FROM GOD:

♥ "For such persons do not serve our Lord Christ, but their own appetites, and by smooth talk and flattery they deceive the hearts of the naive" (Romans 16:18 ESV).

♥ "They profess to know God, but they deny him by their works. They are detestable, disobedient, unfit for any good work" (Titus 1:16 ESV).

GO AHEAD—ANSWER:

»—→ If you were to stand up in front of a crowd and read out loud the things you were posting online, how would it make you look?

»—→ When do you post? When you're sad? Happy? Wanting to brag? What are you hoping for?

»—→ How can you honor God with your social media? What changes do you need to make in what you post?

FROM KRISTIN:

Social media has become an idol in many people's (including adults') lives and eats away time you could be spending doing productive things. I highly suggest taking frequent social media "fasts."

26.
Find a mentor.

Ask someone you respect and who has a strong walk with the Lord to mentor you if no one falls into that place naturally.

Hopefully you're **hanging out** with Christians of all ages, but you'll want to find someone who can walk with you **closely**.

Jesus loved and ministered to all, but He had twelve disciples whom He taught more personally. He **invested** in their spiritual walk and **equipped** them to take over His ministry after His death and resurrection.

People take internships and apprenticeships to learn a craft. They shadow people who are **experienced** and knowledgeable about what they want to learn.

Think of this as **a spiritual** internship. Your mentor won't be perfect, but she'll probably have some valuable **wisdom** she's willing to share. She can offer treasured advice, **perspective**, and correction.

Ask a woman who's older than you if she'd be willing to meet with you once a month and disciple you. Pick someone who is respected, not prone to **gossip** (if you're telling her your problems, you don't want her repeating them to everyone!), and someone with good **character**.

Read scripture together, pray together, and let her give you godly advice. Allow her to hold you **accountable** in reading your Bible, serving, and growing closer to Christ.

You may already have someone in this place. It might be your mom, **a youth leader**, or a family friend. Sometimes, though, you have to ask.

Try to place yourself with someone who does **well** what you're trying to do. For example, if you want to learn how to show **mercy**, pick someone who organizes meals for new mothers and the elderly and help her out.

Want to **prepare for marriage** and family life? Hang around with someone who's been happily married for fifteen years and watch how she treats her husband and kids.

Want to learn how to **serve** faithfully? Offer to help out the church secretary a few hours a week.

Kristin

- -

FROM GOD:

- ❤ "Older women likewise are to be reverent in behavior, not slanderers or slaves to much wine. They are to teach what is good, and so train the young women to love their husbands and children" (Titus 2:3–4 ESV).
- ❤ "And he gave the apostles, the prophets, the evangelists, the shepherds and teachers, to equip the saints for the work of ministry, for building up the body of Christ" (Ephesians 4:11–12 ESV).

GO AHEAD—ANSWER:

- »→ Think of three things you first want to ask your mentor about. What are they?
- »→ List two or three people who could mentor you. Prayerfully consider asking one of them to be part of your life in this way.
- »→ Where do you feel like God is calling you to serve? Is there someone you know who could help you learn how to work in that area of ministry?

FROM KRISTIN:

Some of my best friends are ten or twenty years older than me! I value and treasure their wisdom, encouragement, and support.

FROM SUSIE:

Hey! Are you calling me old?

27.
Accept and love how God made you.

Freckles. Nose **slightly** bent. Little feet. Long fingers. Be **grateful** for everything that makes you *you*!

Instead of feeling **negative** about features you don't like, learn to embrace them. For example, can you imagine actor Owen Wilson without his nose being crooked, or Barbra Streisand and Sarah Jessica Parker without their big noses? Obviously, they learned to **embrace** these less desirable features and use them for their advantage.

Are you familiar with Nick Vujicic? He's an international speaker and recently married, but he has no arms or legs. This guy never let what he *doesn't* have stop him from **having fun**. He has played football, surfed, and enjoyed a variety of other sports. At seventeen years of age, he formed a nonprofit organization called Life without Limbs, and he now travels the world sharing his faith in Christ.

Seventeen-year-old Jordan recently walked into my office wearing a cute T-shirt and a long skirt. She was articulate and very friendly. When I asked her to tell me about herself, she lifted her skirt to her knees, revealing two prosthetic feet and legs. "I have fake feet and legs," she said with ease. Then she **laughed** and said, "You know the best thing about having fake feet? If I find a pair of shoes I love, but they're not available in my size, I can simply adjust my feet to fit any shoe in the world!" Then she proceeded to show me how to make her feet larger or smaller.

This young lady was **amazing**. Instead of complaining about what she didn't have, she made the best of it! People are drawn to these kinds of students. We love being around people who like themselves, are comfortable with themselves, and don't complain about their differences.

Make a decision right now to start liking **ALL** of you! God created you as a unique individual. Embrace that! Revel in the fact that you are part of His very image and likeness!

Susie

• •

FROM GOD:

- ❤ "For you created my inmost being; you knit me together in my mother's womb. I praise you because I am fearfully and wonderfully made; your works are wonderful, I know that full well" (Psalm 139:13–14 NIV).
- ❤ "So God created mankind in his own image, in the image of God he created them; male and female he created them" (Genesis 1:27 NIV).

GO AHEAD—ANSWER:

- »→ We're asked a serious question in Isaiah 45:9–19. Read and discuss this passage now and answer the question.
- »→ Begin filling your mind with positive thoughts about yourself. Go ahead and try it right now. Tell yourself two things you love about you!
- »→ Ask God to teach you to see yourself through His eyes.

FROM SUSIE:

I'm short and squatty. On a good day—if I stretch really high—I'm 5'3". Normal days display my true height at 5'2½". I'd love to be taller, but I'm actually okay being short. I love basketball and have a half-court in my backyard with an in-ground Goalrilla basketball system. Because of the adjustable height flexibility, I can actually dunk!

28.
Take care of yourself by adopting good health habits now.

Take a second to mentally prepare yourself for some earth-shattering news.

Are you ready? You sure?

Okay. Here it is: **You won't be young forever.**

Take a couple of deep breaths. **It'll be okay.**

Lord willing, you'll live a full, long life. If you start bad habits **now**, though, they'll only get **harder** to break as you get older. Bad habits can affect the quality and longevity of your life.

Taking care of your body glorifies God. After all, it belongs to Him!

First, take care of yourself **physically** to the **best of your resources and ability**. You don't have to be a vegan triathlete to live a healthy life. Instead, take little steps toward good health. **Limit junk food.** Add a fruit or vegetable to each meal. **Go for a walk.** Sign up for a sports club. **Shower.** Get to bed at a reasonable hour.

Next, take care of your **mind**. Always be on guard against mental laziness and stay away from **brain candy**. Brain candy is anything **lacking real substance**. **Tabloids**, romance books, and most television shows are examples of brain candy. They're like mental Pixy Stix. They require **no** mental energy to digest, and the content lingers, causing **rot**.

Instead of "bingeing" on an entire afternoon of your favorite mellow drama, pick up a good book, do a **puzzle**, start a craft, learn a language, **go for a jog**, get a part-time job, get ahead on your homework, play with your siblings, **watch a classic movie**, watch a documentary, bake something, write a play, start writing a novel, or do something that requires a little effort on your part.

Finally, and **most importantly**, take care of your **soul**. Your body will eventually die, no matter how well you take care of it. **Your soul won't.** Sow into what lasts for eternity! Stay in the Word, pray, go to church, sing worship songs, and invest in biblical community.

Kristin

FROM GOD:

- ❤ "For while bodily training is of some value, godliness is of value in every way, as it holds promise for the present life and also for the life to come" (1 Timothy 4:8 ESV).
- ❤ "Or do you not know that your body is a temple of the Holy Spirit within you, whom you have from God? You are not your own, for you were bought with a price. So glorify God in your body" (1 Corinthians 6:19–20 ESV).

GO AHEAD—ANSWER:

- »→ What're some areas where you struggle to take care of yourself? What's at the root of those struggles?
- »→ Think of three small changes you can make to live a healthier life.
- »→ Do you think God cares about our health habits? Why or why not?

FROM KRISTIN:

Sometimes all it takes is one or two small actions to get you going. Try drinking a glass of water first thing in the morning or taking a short walk when you get home from school each day.

29.
Know that God's discipline means He loves you.

If you've never read the **Old Testament**, I encourage you to read it. Many of the people were flakes. . .kind of like us. They'd get really excited about serving God, then something else would capture their attention, and they'd wander away. God would bring them back; they'd wander away. **Again and again.**

As you read the **Old Testament**, you'll notice there are several tribes: the Israelites (God's chosen people), the Edomites (wicked people who died off), the Levites (a tribe of the Israelites where the priests came from), the Mosquito Bites (we're still asking why God created them), and the Pepsi-Lites.

Each time the people wandered away from God, He **disciplined** them. Why? Because He loved them. You see, a God who doesn't really care doesn't bother with discipline. But our God—who truly loves you—**cares about you too much** to allow you to stay the way you are. He's going to prove His love for you by transforming you, **breaking you**, and remaking you in His image—to reflect His goodness.

I used to have a 160-pound St. Bernard named Bosco. Before he came to live with me, I decided I didn't want him on the **furniture**. But once he got on the furniture, it was kind of cute, so I took photos and let him stay on the couch.

Not long after, he was on my bed. And he was taking up more space than he should have! Bosco had the covers and the **center** of the bed, while I barely hung on to the side. And he finally took over the whole house. Meaning, I was a terrible disciplinarian. He ruled the house.

I probably should've taken him to **obedience** school. I probably should've demanded that he get off the furniture and stop chewing my shoes. I probably should've taken **myself** to obedience school! But it was just too much work.

We should **celebrate** the fact that we serve a God who's willing to invest the time it takes to train us, reshape us, and teach us how to reflect His glory. Part of His investment in us is the discipline He uses on us.

When we need to seek **forgiveness** from someone, He nudges our heart and prods us forward. Other times He'll use His Holy Spirit to sear our conscience and let us know we've gone against His will.

Be glad when God disciplines, because it proves **two** things:

He's working in your life.

He sees greater potential in you.

The fact that He sees **possibility** in you means that He's dreaming **bigger** for you than you're dreaming for yourself! While you only see the immediate, He's looking into your future and seeing all that you can **become**! So bring on the discipline—it's His loving way of preparing you for all He has in store.

Susie

. . . .

FROM GOD:

- ❤ "My son, *do not make light of* the Lord's discipline, and do not lose heart when he rebukes you, because the Lord disciplines the one he loves. . ." (Hebrews 12:5–6 NIV, emphasis mine).
- ❤ "Whoever loves discipline loves knowledge, but whoever hates correction is stupid" (Proverbs 12:1 NIV).

GO AHEAD—ANSWER:

- »→ Describe a time when you were disciplined by your parents. How did this affect you?
- »→ Describe someone who's spoiled. How would proper discipline change his/her life?
- »→ How does being disciplined as a child or teenager prepare us for the future?

FROM SUSIE:

How we accept discipline is often a reflection of our maturity level. One who is teachable can go a long way. But someone who gets defensive when being disciplined might as well be saying, "Wah, wah, wah. I'm such a baby. The world is supposed to revolve around me!"

30.

If everyone jumps off a bridge, find out why they're jumping.

If everyone jumped off a bridge, would you?

It seems you can't get through your teen years without getting asked this question.

You're supposed to answer no, but if everyone's jumping off a bridge, I'm going to find out *why*. Because if *everyone's* doing it, *maybe* there's a good reason.

Perhaps we've prematurely judged jumping off bridges. Perhaps there's a gigantic fire sweeping the entire land and the only way to escape is to jump off a bridge into a lake. Or maybe the zombie apocalypse started and we discover zombies can't swim so we're forced to jump off bridges to get to safety.

Or maybe everyone's simply showing off and doing flips off a bridge and onto the pavement. You don't have any gymnastics training and flipping off the bridge would almost guarantee a broken neck. When you don't jump, you're teased and called a chicken. (To which you should respond: "Thank you. Despite the stereotype, chickens are actually quite bold.") Still, don't jump off the bridge.

There are two main trains of thought:

Thought Train #1: If something's popular, it **must** be bad. Therefore I'm going to avoid it.

Thought Train #2: If something's popular, it **must** be amazing and I'm missing out by avoiding it.

Rather than jumping on or off a bandwagon too quickly, **start thinking for yourself**. Take each trend, fad, and bandwagon and weigh it against what you **know is true**. Don't let your peers do your thinking for you.

Is the television show everyone's talking about honoring to God? Does the content of that new book make you think about sin and its consequences? Does it motivate you to action? Or does it make you desire sin? Do you *know* the party everyone's going to will have alcohol and drugs?

There are numerous popular television shows and movies **famous** for their sharp writing, good plot, and strong character development. There're tons of books that are **exciting** without being graphic or indecent. There are ways to have **fun** without going to an out-of-control party.

If your parents ask you not to watch a certain movie, read a certain book, or stay away from certain places, **politely** ask them their reasons. If they don't tell you, though, knowing they've got your best interest at heart is enough reason to avoid something.

Kristin

• •

FROM GOD:

♥ "And it is my prayer that your love may abound more and more, with knowledge and all discernment, so that you may approve what is excellent, and so be pure and blameless for the day of Christ" (Philippians 1:9–10 ESV).

♥ "Do not judge by appearances, but judge with right judgment" (John 7:24 ESV).

GO AHEAD—ANSWER:

»—→ Do you find it hard to resist things that are popular? Or do you try to be "cool" by doing the opposite of everyone else?

»—→ Why do you think God tells us to discern?

»—→ What are some ways we can look to God to determine whether something is popular for good or bad reasons?

FROM KRISTIN:

At the end of the day, it's important to learn to discern. And if you rhyme in the process, so much the better!

31.

Put away your phone and spend time with the people you're with.

Want to know a fast way to show someone you don't care about them?

Pull out your cell phone and start texting or surfing the web while they're talking to you.

Constantly having your phone out while you're with others sends some powerful silent messages.

It says:

- My business is more important than you.
- You're boring.
- I wish I were somewhere else.
- I don't value you.

You may not be thinking those things, but that's how your behavior comes across.

We've become so saturated with technology that people can't go two minutes without checking their phone. We're so consumed with our online "friends and followers" that we miss out on developing rich, meaningful friendships with **real, live human beings**.

It's a hard habit to break, so here are some tips for success:

- When you get together with someone, **put your phone** where you won't be tempted to look at it.
- When at home, put your phone in one spot so that you have to travel a distance to check it. Don't keep it with you constantly.
- If you *do* need to check your phone while talking with someone, politely excuse yourself and say something like, "I'm so sorry, I need to respond to this text real quick."
- Consider *not* getting a smartphone. I know, I know. That's our culture's equivalent of **living in a cave**, but living in a cave can be fun!

Kristin

FROM GOD:

- ❤ "Do nothing out of selfish ambition or vain conceit. Rather, in humility value others above yourselves" (Philippians 2:3 NIV).
- ❤ "To one who listens, valid criticism is like a gold earring or other gold jewelry" (Proverbs 25:12 NLT).

GO AHEAD—ANSWER:

- »—→ How does it make you feel when someone constantly interrupts a conversation with you to text or check their phone?
- »—→ Phones aren't bad, but they can be used badly. What are some bad uses of your phone?
- »—→ Can you think of ways to use your phone positively?

FROM KRISTIN:

I still have a flip phone. (I like being on the cutting edge of ten-year-old technology.) My outdated phone has started more conversations with random strangers than anything else!

FROM SUSIE:

I think it would be awesome if someone could create a phone we couldn't lose...like...I don't know...maybe a phone we could actually attach to the wall. Then we wouldn't have to carry it around with us. Wouldn't that be awesome? We'd just leave it at home—on the wall. And we'd never lose it!

32.
Ask for forgiveness.

When I (Susie) was growing up, my brother and I were taught to say, "Will you forgive me?" instead of "I'm sorry" whenever we hurt each other's feelings or did something wrong. It's much more **humbling** to ask, "Will you forgive me?" than simply spitting out a halfhearted apology.

"I'm sorry" has become cliché. "**Sorry.** Sorry 'bout that. Sorry I stepped on your foot. Sorry I cut you off in line. Sorry. Sorry that's how you took it." It has just become **too easy** to say. We say it almost without even thinking.

But to seek forgiveness from someone requires **humility**.

It tears down walls.

It **bridges gaps**.

It restores wholeness.

I wonder how many marriages could be saved if both parties were willing to seek forgiveness from one another?

It's sad, but because seeking revenge has become more popular than mending relationships or building bridges, we seldom hear someone ask, "Will you forgive me?" Seeking forgiveness is admitting we're wrong. It goes against our natural grain.

The Holy Spirit working within us, though, can teach us humility and help us seek forgiveness from those we have hurt.

When should you ask for forgiveness?

Whenever the situation is 1 percent your fault. If you're even a little to blame, go ahead and accept responsibility, humble yourself, and seek forgiveness.

What if he or she refuses to forgive?

If you've asked from a genuine heart—you truly meant it—then you've done all you need to do. The problem now lies with the other person. You're free.

Susie

FROM GOD:

- ♥ "Therefore, if you are offering your gift at the altar and there remember that your brother or sister has something against you, leave your gift there in front of the altar. First go and be reconciled to them; then come and offer your gift" (Matthew 5:23–24 NIV).
- ♥ "For if you forgive other people when they sin against you, your heavenly Father will also forgive you" (Matthew 6:14 NIV).

GO AHEAD—ANSWER:

- »→ Has anyone ever asked you to forgive him? Have you ever asked anyone to forgive you? If so, how did that make you feel? If not, why haven't you?
- »→ What's the biggest difference in saying you're sorry and seeking forgiveness?
- »→ Ask God if there's anyone with whom you need to seek forgiveness.

FROM SUSIE:

Someone who's teachable—someone who can admit it when she's wrong—will always be more successful, have more friends, and be happier than someone who's always right.

33.
Give yourself to Christ.

Did you know that God is your biggest **cheerleader**? He thinks about you constantly—as in 24-7. . .365. Seriously! **Here's the proof:** "How precious it is, Lord, to realize that you are thinking about me constantly!" (Psalm 139:17 TLB).

He **loves you** more than you can comprehend. His love for you is immeasurable. **Beyond your imagination.** That's why He sent His only Son, Jesus Christ, to die for you. And when did He do this?

According to the Bible, He did it while you were still a stinkin' sinner: "But God demonstrates his own love for us in this: While we were still sinners, Christ died for us" (Romans 5:8 NIV). Wow! That's a lot of love.

Someone had to **pay the penalty** for your sin—and **you** were in line to pay for it. *How much is the penalty for sin?* It's a lot. It's death! **Here's the proof:** "For the wages of sin is death" (Romans 6:23 NIV).

God loves you so much that He sent His Son, Jesus, to die **for** you so you could escape the death penalty! **What an amazing gift.** But—like any gift—you have to accept it in order to get it.

Accepting the free gift of **forgiveness** for sins means you have to recognize the fact that you're a sinner. We were born sinners. So the question is: **Have you asked Christ to forgive your sins?** When I realized His great love for me, I fell in love with Him! And I placed my **faith** in Him and began to live for Him. But **first** I had to seek His forgiveness. So I prayed and asked Him to forgive my sins. **He did.**

And He'll forgive yours, too, if you'll ask Him. **Here's the proof:** "If we confess our sins, he is faithful and just and will forgive us our sins and purify us from all unrighteousness" (1 John 1:9 NIV).

If you'd like to ask forgiveness for your sins, you can pray the prayer listed on page 219.

Is that all?

No. This is only the beginning! Don't think of prayer as your ticket to heaven; it doesn't work that way. You have to actually *mean* the words—they have to come from your heart—when you pray them. And after He has forgiven your sins, you're a **Christian**. And this is where the **adventure** begins!

Now you'll want to actually **grow** spiritually. Right now you're a new Christian. A baby Christian. To mature in your faith requires growing up (see next tip). And you can start right now by getting involved in a church and a **youth group**.

Find a church that preaches the Bible and has an active youth group or Bible study, and get plugged in.

Also, talk with the pastor about getting **baptized**. Jesus set the example for us when He was baptized, and we want to follow His example in **everything** we do.

One more thing: Now that you're a Christian, tell someone! Go ahead. **It's not a secret.**

Susie

• •

FROM GOD:

♥ "For the wages of sin is death, but the gift of God is eternal life in Christ Jesus our Lord" (Romans 6:23 NIV).

♥ "Now God says he will accept and acquit us—declare us 'not guilty'—if we trust Jesus Christ to take away our sins. And we all can be saved in this same way, by coming to Christ, no matter who we are or what we have been like" (Romans 3:22 TLB).

GO AHEAD—ANSWER:

»—→ How does it make you feel to know that eternal life, forgiveness for sins. . .salvation is a free gift from God? How are you responding to God?

»—→ Have you trusted Christ to take away your sins?

»—→ Have you actually walked away from a sinful lifestyle?

FROM SUSIE:

Giving my life to Christ was the best decision I've ever made! No regrets. And it just keeps getting better. His faithfulness amazes me.

FROM KRISTIN:

After becoming a Christian, it's neat to look back on your life and see where God had His hand in it—even before you put your trust in Him!

34.
Grow in Christ.

After you've given your life to Christ, you'll want to make sure you grow up spiritually. You wouldn't want to remain a **baby girl** forever, and God doesn't want you to remain as a baby Christian.

Physical growth and spiritual growth actually have a lot in common. Both require the right **nutrition**. To grow strong bones, you need the right nourishment. To grow strong spiritually, you need to feed on the **Bible**. God's Word is filled with the nutrients you need to enable your faith to grow.

Surround yourself with **people** who will encourage you spiritually. Steer away from negative influences. People who pressure you to do things that will damage your faith should be avoided. Choose to **involve yourself** in church, a growing youth group, and a Bible study. These involvements will teach you how to **study the Bible** and apply it to your life.

You'll also want to learn how to share your faith. Think about what you have! You possess the **secret** to living forever in paradise. You have a genuine relationship with the Creator of the universe! You'll get to live eternally with Him! Share this knowledge with others, and try to tell as many people as you can about what Jesus has done for you and the Kingdom of God.

Susie

• •

FROM GOD:

❤ "But grow in the grace and knowledge of our Lord and Savior Jesus Christ. To him be glory both now and forever! Amen" (2 Peter 3:18 NIV).

❤ "And this is my prayer: that your love may abound more and more in knowledge and depth of insight, so that you may be able to discern what is best and may be pure and blameless for the day of Christ, filled with the fruit of righteousness that comes through Jesus Christ—to the glory and praise of God" (Philippians 1:9–11 NIV).

GO AHEAD—ANSWER:

»—→ What evidence do you see in someone's life who is growing spiritually?

»—→ What are some things that keep us from growing spiritually?

»—→ What specifically do you need to do to grow spiritually?

FROM SUSIE:

I've learned it's impossible to grow spiritually without reading the Bible. We can listen to Christian music every day, take notes during great sermons, and be involved in church and youth group. But unless we actually spend time each day reading God's Word, we won't actually "grow up" spiritually.

Have you ever desired to **sing and tap-dance** in the rain? If not, then you probably haven't watched *Singin' in the Rain*, one of my favorite classic films.

Or have you invested four hours of your life in Scarlett O'Hara and Rhett Butler's drama as they work out their flaws during the Civil War–era classic *Gone with the Wind*?

Do you know which movie generated the popular idea that every time a bell rings, an angel gets its wings? (*It's a Wonderful Life*)

Classic movies contain certain elements lacking from most of today's films, such as character development and a plot. Nowadays it's just a bunch of unrealistically perfect-looking people running around half naked blowing things up.

Movie standards have become **increasingly relaxed** in recent years. High-tech special effects have replaced an actual story line, explicit romance and flippant dialogue have been put in place of character development, and stories rarely reflect any moral truth, except that you should do whatever makes you feel good. The desire to **shock an audience** and "push boundaries" has trumped the need to make a film that challenges an audience to think. We're living in an age where **everything is flashy** and on-demand, and we're constantly trying to outdo the last epic adventure.

Do a Google search of the most popular classic movies to find what's out there. You can also ask your grandparents or mom and dad for their recommendations. They might even have some cool stories to share if they were around when the movies came out!

Some of my favorites are: *The Three Musketeers* (the one with Gene Kelly), *Meet Me in St. Louis*, *Anne of Green Gables*, and, of course, the aforementioned *Singin' in the Rain*. Whenever it starts raining I have to resist the urge to stop everything I'm doing and go outside to do a little soft-shoe. (Soft-shoe is a tap-dance style, and I know approximately three steps. But really, **three is all you need** to put on a complete song-and-dance number.)

Before buying anything, check with your local library. They'll probably have a lot of these classics in stock.

Kristin

FROM GOD:

- ♥ "Keep your heart with all vigilance, for from it flow the springs of life" (Proverbs 4:23 ESV).
- ♥ "Abstain from the things polluted by idols, and from sexual immorality, and from what has been strangled, and from blood" (Acts 15:20 ESV).

GO AHEAD—ANSWER:

»—→ Have you seen any classic movies? Which ones?

»—→ What did you like about them? Did you dislike anything about them?

»—→ Why should we be careful about the underlying messages of movies?

FROM KRISTIN:

I like to keep an eye out for movies releasing today that'll be considered classics for my grandchildren. I hope they'll watch The Chronicles of Narnia and Lord of the Rings and say," Wow! My grandma was alive when these were made!"

36.

Turn off the television and try something new!

I learned how to make *amazing* milkshakes and malts this year! Now all my friends want me to make them one. I also designed and converted my *upstairs loft* into a Coca-Cola café! I flip burgers, grill cheese sandwiches, and pour iced Coca-Cola at countless **parties**. And it all happened because I was willing to turn off the TV for a while.

It's amazing what you can accomplish if you're willing to go **without** TV for a bit. Are there some things in the back of your mind that you've wanted to get done but just never seem to have the time? Maybe it's cleaning out your closet, planning a **garage sale**, trying a new recipe, learning ventriloquism, or redecorating your bedroom. Give yourself a time frame, and make a schedule of what you'll get accomplished on each day. **Stick with it.** Then take photos and post them on Facebook so we can celebrate with you!

(You can check out my Coca-Cola café on my website: SusieShellenberger.com.)

It really comes down to **priorities**, doesn't it? Have you ever wondered how things might be different if the early Christians had TV or the Internet to **compete** for their time and attention?

Picture Jesus waiting to be baptized by John the Baptist.

JESUS: John?

JOHN: Just a sec, Jesus. I'm getting a text.

Or. . .

JESUS: Let's feed the five thousand.

DISCIPLES: Can't. No food.

ANDREW: I found a boy with some bread and fish.

JESUS: Bring the boy to Me.

ANDREW: I can't right now. I'm bidding on a new fishing pole on eBay.

Thankfully, the disciples weren't distracted with modern technology. We can't afford to be distracted by it either. Yes, we need it. But we can't allow it to become more important than doing things that need to get done.

So go ahead. Turn off the TV for a while. Make a list of some things you'd love to do. I'll get you started:

- Start a Bible study.
- Learn sign language.
- Rent a tandem bicycle and take a friend for a ride and a picnic.

- Start a blog.
- Create a newsletter for your youth group.
- Camp out in your backyard.
- Make your own movie.
- Write your own novel.
- Learn to count to ten in Amharic, Creole, Swahili, and Thai.
- Create a new app.

Who knows? You may accomplish so much while the TV is off, you'll make a million dollars! (If you do, please purchase a copy of this book for everyone in Rhode Island.)

Susie

FROM GOD:

♥ "Laziness casts one into a deep sleep, and an idle person will suffer hunger" (Proverbs 19:15 NKJV).

♥ "Lazy hands make for poverty, but diligent hands bring wealth" (Proverbs 10:4 NIV).

GO AHEAD—ANSWER:

»→ What are some things you watch on TV that you could easily do without? Will you do it for one week?

»→ How much extra time would you have if you actually gave up TV for a week?

»→ What specifically can you imagine God doing in and through you in one week if you're willing to give up TV and ask Him to direct you to something amazing?

FROM SUSIE:

I'm headed upstairs to my Coca-Cola café to make a chocolate malt with Whoppers and Cool Whip on top. And whatever TV shows I have to miss for this is totally worth it.

37.
Write letters.

This was before your time, but there **was** a day when women actually made soap, kneaded dough, **washed clothes by hand**, wore girdles, shared a phone line with neighbors, hung wet clothes on lines outside to dry, sent thank-you cards, and wrote letters.

Unfortunately, letter writing has become a lost art. Why take the time to write an actual letter when you can simply text or e-mail someone the same information? (The answer is actually in the question. **Because it takes time.**)

When you receive a letter, it means someone actually took the time to sit down and write it! Someone thought enough of you to search for a funny card she thought you'd enjoy, write a note inside, purchase a stamp, and even mail it! We pay in time **and** money.

When I was growing up, it was the highlight of my day to get a letter in the mail from my cousin. It wasn't the content that was so special—it was the fact that she stopped doing whatever she was doing and made time to think about me. It was the fact that something arrived in our mailbox with my name on it! Something came just for me!

Amidst the bills, advertisements, catalogs, and brochures, a letter stood out in the pile for me. I felt **special**, recognized, wanted, loved.

My brother and I were taught to send thank-you notes each Christmas and birthday to the people who had given us gifts. I'm so glad I learned that as a child because now it's **seared** into my brain: thank the people who are kind to you! It's important to let them know I appreciate what they did for me.

It's easy to feel **taken advantage of** when we give a gift and the recipient never acknowledges it, never expresses gratitude for our efforts. Of course, if the reason you're giving is because you want to be noticed, then you need to examine your motives. We should give simply because we want to. Christ gave **extravagantly**, and we want to imitate Him.

Take some time this week to send handwritten note cards or letters. Strive to write and mail two a day. Send notes of **encouragement** to your pastors, your relatives, and those who are making a positive difference in your life. Consider writing thank-you cards to your immediate family members (you don't have to mail these!). Go ahead—make someone's day!

Susie

FROM GOD:

- ❤ "Be kind and compassionate to one another. . ." (Ephesians 4:32 NIV).
- ❤ "Let us not become weary in doing good, for at the proper time we will reap a harvest if we do not give up" (Galatians 6:9 NIV).
- ❤ "But encourage one another daily, as long as it is called 'Today,' so that none of you may be hardened by sin's deceitfulness" (Hebrews 3:13 NIV).

GO AHEAD—ANSWER:

⟫—→ When was the last time you sent a thank-you note? What was it for?

⟫—→ Will you send a handwritten note to someone this week?

FROM SUSIE:

When I was in grade school, I used clothespins to attach playing cards to the spokes on my bicycle wheels to make it sound like my bike had a motor when I rode it. So cool!

38.

Take a moment to enjoy the "little things."

As a kid, if I got too busy, my grandmother would say, **"Stop and smell the flowers."** This is an old-fashioned saying meaning we need to stop being so consumed with life and just live.

The world is a go-go-go place. That's why it's important to learn to take moments throughout the day and reflect on the beauty and intricacy of the world around you.

You may not always have time to go on a long hike, spend hours staring at the stars, or sit in a park and enjoy a picnic, but you can still enjoy the beauty in the little things around you if you know how to look.

So what are these "little things"?

A mother walking hand-in-hand down the sidewalk with her young daughter.

The sun breaking through the clouds onto the road.

Cows relaxing in a green pasture.

An elderly couple rocking on their porch, waving as you drive by.

The man at the airport who assists a disabled woman.

The incredible cloud formations underneath your plane as it soars seven miles above the earth.

Looking up to see the brightness of the stars and moon as you run back out to the car to get the book you forgot.

Those are just a few of the infinite tiny moments of beauty we can cherish in a day. These moments make the days richer and your heart more joyous.

Be on the lookout. They're everywhere!

Kristin

• •

FROM GOD:

❤ "He has made everything beautiful in its time" (Ecclesiastes 3:11 ESV).

❤ "The earth is the LORD's and the fullness thereof, the world and those who dwell therein" (Psalm 24:1 ESV).

GO AHEAD—ANSWER:

»——→ What small things bring you joy during the day?

»——→ Do you take time to enjoy little things throughout the day?
What does it do to your mood?

»——→ Tomorrow make a point to look for little moments of beauty.
Share what you saw with someone!

FROM KRISTIN:

I may be one of the few people who loves sitting in airports. There are so many fascinating moments to watch as peoples' lives briefly intersect.

Have you ever heard the saying, "Birds of a feather flock together"? **It's true.** You never see an eagle and a sparrow flying together. Or a tiger and an armadillo developing a friendship. Imagine a duck and an elephant sharing living quarters! We tend to gravitate toward those who are most like us.

Many times girls date and marry an alcoholic because their dad was an alcoholic. This is what they're familiar with. **It's what they know.** And oftentimes you'll notice really smart people hanging out with other brainiacs. It's because these are the people with whom they're comfortable.

So if you want to be wise, choose friends who make **wise** choices. Check out what Proverbs 13:20 says: "Be with wise men and become wise. Be with evil men and become evil" (TLB).

If you want to learn about politics, become a page, get a job at the state capitol, read. If NASCAR interests you, go to the races. Get to know the people behind the scenes. If it's fashion you're into, try to shadow a buyer for a large store.

We can't help but pick up on **what's happening** around us. Sure, you can go to a party where drugs are prevalent and refrain, but why even place yourself in that situation? The wise person **thinks** ahead and plays out the scenario in his or her mind. Knowing there'll be people in attendance who will **pressure** you to drink, choose ahead of time to stay away.

Christ's disciples hung together and became so spiritually strong they were able to birth the New Church. One way to enhance your **spiritual growth** is to hang out with other Christians. Become active in a Bible study. Seek out Christians at school.

Let's get back to becoming wise. When seeking out wise people, keep in mind that **wisdom** comes in many shapes and sizes. The old lady in your church who never comes to church anymore because she's confined in an assisted living place probably has a lot to offer. Be willing to **seek out** people like this. And be patient. Because when she says, "Eow's oh I uhrnd to hee Bahd's juice" what she's really saying is, "Here's how I learned to hear God's voice." But because she may be missing a few teeth, you'll want to be a patient listener and take notes.

Susie

FROM GOD:

- ❤ Getting wisdom is the most important thing you can do! And with your wisdom, develop common sense and good judgment" (Proverbs 4:7 TLB).
- ❤ "A life of doing right is the wisest life there is" (Proverbs 4:11 TLB).

GO AHEAD—ANSWER:

»—→ Describe someone you know who's really wise.

»—→ Discuss the difference between wisdom and intelligence.

»—→ What's the wisest decision you've ever made?

FROM SUSIE:

I've discovered wisdom is also learned through listening. The less I talk and the more I listen... my chances of becoming wise double!

40.
Take responsibility for your actions.

When you're caught doing something wrong, do you **blame** someone or something else for **causing** you to sin? In order to grow and mature, you must start taking responsibility for your actions.

In this life, you *will* be wronged. People will get angry with you, lie to you, gossip about you, lash out at you, steal from you, and manipulate you. Hurt is very real, and the evil people inflict on one another is horrific. (And remember—never stay in any situation where you're being routinely hurt. Get out and get help!)

Don't use an offense as an excuse to sin. A **reason** for bad behavior is not an **excuse for it**.

By **recognizing** and taking **responsibility** for your *own* actions, you can often prevent more hurt.

- **Don't lie to people**, even if you've been lied to a thousand times.
- **Be kind with your words**, even if people have said nasty things to you.
- **Don't gossip**, even if your entire school is talking about you behind your back.
- **Stay calm**, even if everyone around you is angry.
- **Don't take things from others**, even if people have taken things from you.

When (notice I didn't say *if*) you sin, **immediately** confess and repent. Accept any consequences for your actions. While you can't control the actions of others, you *can* control your own actions. You are **responsible** for only yourself, and believe me, that'll be enough to keep you busy!

Kristin

• •

FROM GOD:

♥ "Let no one say when he is tempted, 'I am being tempted by God,' for God cannot be tempted with evil, and he himself tempts no one. But each person is tempted when he is lured and enticed by his own desire" (James 1:13–14 ESV).

♥ "If we confess our sins, he is faithful and just to forgive us our sins and to cleanse us from all unrighteousness" (1 John 1:9 ESV).

GO AHEAD—ANSWER:

»→ What's your reaction when you get caught doing wrong?

»→ What does it say to those around us when we never recognize our faults? What does it say to God?

»→ What do you think would happen if you admitted your shortcomings and tried to change?

FROM KRISTIN:

God loves a humble heart. So if you've messed up, take ownership of the mistake and be truly sorry. God's already forgiven you, and He'll be faithful to continue the work He started in you.

41.
Have a junk e-mail account.

Have you ever put your e-mail down to sign up for something and suddenly you started receiving **billions** of random e-mails promoting products like cruises to the Cayman Islands and sneakers that'll make you look 45 percent more awesome when you run?

If so, you've become the victim of **junk e-mail**, or spam. Spam is the scourge of the digital age, and it usually happens to people at least a dozen times a day. To prevent this annoying little corruption from happening to you, I recommend you set up a junk e-mail account.

Use **this e-mail** when you. . .

- sign up to receive coupons.
- join any kind of online group.
- sign up for social media and don't want to get an e-mail every time someone posts something.
- join restaurant birthday clubs. (Just remember to check your junk e-mail around your birthday so you can get all those awesome free-food coupons!)
- apply for your reward cards at stores.
- aren't sure something is reputable.
- enter contests (Just don't put personal information!)
- really are the one-thousandth viewer and will get a free iPad. Just in case.
- suspect anything else that might bombard you with spam.

Kristin

* *

FROM GOD:

♥ "Who is like the wise? And who knows the interpretation of a thing? A man's wisdom makes his face shine, and the hardness of his face is changed" (Ecclesiastes 8:1 ESV).

♥ "Listen to advice and accept instruction, that you may gain wisdom in the future" (Proverbs 19:20 ESV).

GO AHEAD—ANSWER:

»—→ Have you received lots of junk e-mail?

»—→ This isn't really a moralistic "right or wrong" issue. What are some other things that aren't necessarily right or wrong, but one thing may be the smarter choice?

»—→ So, what's your junk e-mail address?

FROM KRISTIN:

My dad created a spam e-mail account for our family called webercrud@verizon.net. Do you think people suspect we're giving them a junk e-mail address?

42.
Spend time outside.

Have you ever stepped outside on a crisp fall day and watched the sunlight catch the fiery red leaves as the cool breeze strokes your face, hinting at the coming season change?

Or stepped outside right after a storm and inhaled the fresh scent of rain while watching the dark billowing clouds roll away?

When was the last time you gazed up at the stars and considered that God placed them there and knows each one by name?

Spending time outside is good for both your body and soul.

Being outside puts life into perspective. It's hard to feel like the center of the universe when you're watching a huge, splendid waterfall crash into a raging river.

The creation stirs our awe and wonder of God. If the majesty of the mountains takes your breath away, how much greater and majestic is the God who formed them? If He takes care of the smallest creatures, providing them with food and shelter, how much more will He take care of His chosen children?

God has revealed Himself through creation. Romans 1:20 tells us God's eternal power and divine nature have been clearly perceived since the creation of the world in the things that were created.

From the dancing stars to the depths of the ocean, creation is shouting at the top of its lungs the glory of its Creator. Are you?

Kristin

• •

FROM GOD:

- ❤ "The heavens declare the glory of God, and the sky above proclaims his handiwork" (Psalm 19:1 ESV).
- ❤ "Let the heavens be glad, and let the earth rejoice; let the sea roar, and all that fills it; let the field exult, and everything in it! Then shall all the trees of the forest sing for joy" (Psalm 96:11–12 ESV).

GO AHEAD—ANSWER:

»——→ What's your favorite thing to do outside?

»——→ Have you seen any natural wonders that have stirred your affections for your Creator?

»——→ Read Psalm 19:1 again. Can you think of other ways nature declares God's glory?

FROM KRISTIN:

One of my favorite things to do is look at the stars. It's hard not to feel the majesty of God when you're looking into the depths of space.

43.

Remember that what you see on TV and in the magazines isn't always real.

Waaaaay back in 1989 a company called Focus on the Family hired me to create a **monthly printed magazine** for teen girls. We called it *Brio*. It was a great magazine, and my staff and I had a blast putting it together each month.

From time to time, our designers did a little Photoshopping. I remember one of our **cover stories** about a championship Jet-Skier. Great photo, but her face was really red from a nasty sunburn. "No problem," our designer said. "We can airbrush the red out of her cheeks." **Problem solved.**

Another cover featured a contemporary Christian music artist with a little strand of **hair** that kind of flew up during the photo shoot. He asked if we could fix it. "Sure," our designer said. **Problem solved.**

Then there was the gal with **crooked** teeth. She had a great story, and we were excited about sharing it. But the teeth took our attention away from the story and forced us to focus on her mouth instead. "No worries," our designer said. "We can fix her teeth." **Problem solved.**

Then we started getting letters from readers who said they felt like **zeroes** because they never looked like anyone in the magazine. They never expected to look like the supermodels featured on secular magazines, but they hoped a **Christian magazine** would feature more normal-looking girls to whom they could relate.

So our staff decided to **stop** airbrushing and Photoshopping. Did every photo have to be perfect? No. What *was* important, we decided, was that our readers be able to relate to the people we put inside our pages.

We decided to do a feature on Photoshopping and airbrushing and expose the deceit behind perfect pictures. We took some photos of girls who were willing to be in the magazine—exactly how they were seen right after getting out of bed. They didn't look good at all—and that's exactly what we wanted!

We then took those **photos** and made them gorgeous, showing our readers exactly what was done at each step. When we were finished, those girls looked like supermodels! And we explained that **anyone** and **anything** can be made to look beautiful.

We warned girls not to compare themselves to who they see on magazine covers because the photos aren't real. They've been airbrushed and Photoshopped until **every blemish**, stray hair, tooth inconsistency, and freckle has been taken care of.

Even the "casual" photos of models wearing worn-out jeans and sporting tousled, slept-in shirts and hair take hours to create the look! So don't fall for it. It's just not real.

I **admire** the celebs who, from time to time, have done television specials without makeup to show the audience what's real and what's not.

Perfect hair, flawless skin, and shiny, super-white teeth aren't real.

Love from your heavenly Father? Very real!

You were created in His image. Can't get more real than that.

Susie

. . . .

FROM GOD:

♥ "I have created you and cared for you since you were born. I will be your God through all your lifetime, yes, even when your hair is white with age. I made you and I will care for you. I will carry you along and be your Savior" (Isaiah 46:3–4 TLB).

♥ "You made all the delicate, inner parts of my body, and knit them together in my mother's womb. Thank you for making me so wonderfully complex! It is amazing to think about. Your workmanship is marvelous" (Psalm 139:13–14 TLB).

GO AHEAD—ANSWER:

»→ Name two physical characteristics you like about yourself.

»→ Describe two things you do well.

»→ Ask God to help you see yourself through His eyes. Ask Him to teach you that He loves you!

FROM SUSIE:

It was my sophomore year of high school. Every single morning, I pulled my bedroom curtains apart, looked up at the sky, and prayed, "Father, teach me that You love me today." WOW! What a difference that made in my life! He did teach me. Every single day, He taught me. And that, in turn, helped me love myself and become confident in who He created me to be.

44.
Write a poem or a song. Rhyming is therapeutic.

One of the most relaxing, challenging, and satisfying hobbies is writing poetry or songs. You don't have to be a famous singer to write songs or a popular poet to eloquently describe the world around you.

Have you ever read through Psalms? It's the long book in the Old Testament, around the middle of your Bible. David and other psalmists use beautiful lyrics and poetry to confess sin, proclaim God's attributes, and prophesy the coming of Jesus.

"For we are his workmanship, created in Christ Jesus for good works, which God prepared beforehand, that we should walk in them" (Ephesians 2:10 ESV).

We're God's workmanship. That means God is crafting, chiseling, painting, writing, and creating you to go forth and do things that He's specifically prepared for you! God has taken what was dead in sin and created it into a beautiful work of art.

Meditate on that for a moment.

Doesn't that make you want to burst into a song of joy?

Because we're made in His image, we have the ability to express the beauty and brokenness of the world into words. Poetry and songs express truths in ways plain words can't capture. They invoke a deep sense of longing and affection for God.

If you play an instrument, try coming up with your own accompaniment. Even better, start a band or worship group with your friends or start a book of poetry.

Kristin

• •

FROM GOD:

- ♥ "I will sing of steadfast love and justice; to you, O Lord, I will make music" (Psalm 101:1 ESV).
- ♥ "It is good to give thanks to the Lord, to sing praises to your name, O Most High" (Psalm 92:1 ESV).

GO AHEAD—ANSWER:

»→ Have you ever written a song? Or poem? What was it about?

»→ How does knowing you're God's workmanship change the way you act?

»→ Read Psalm 92. What did you learn about God in this chapter that could be used for worship?

FROM KRISTIN:

If you're looking for a good place to start, think about God and His attributes or pick a piece of scripture. A lot of great hymns and worship songs are centered on God's greatness or based on a particular Bible verse.

Everyone loves a good **Sunday dinner** of roast beef, mashed potatoes, and green bean casserole. I can smell it now—the roast simmering in the Crock-Pot. . .the aroma **saturating** my home.

Learning how to make a great roast beef dinner will make you popular with your friends when you're out of college and no one can decide on which restaurant to eat at after church, will enable you to give your future family a great Sunday dinner, and will provide a healthy meal with leftovers. And. . .every girl should just know how to make a great **roast beef** dinner!

I make a pretty mean roast. The kind that just falls apart in chunks. This is called chuck roast. The rump roast is the kind that's sliced and—in my opinion —isn't as good, tender, or juicy as the chuck.

I'm going to share a few of my secrets with you, but please don't tell anyone or they won't be secrets anymore.

Secret #1: Ask the meat person at the grocery store to help you select a great chuck roast.

Secret #2: Start preparing Chuck the night before you plan to serve him.

Secret #3: Sear Chuck in a skillet with some flour. Flip him over and sear him with flour on the other side, too.

Secret #4: After ten minutes, move Chuck from the skillet to his new home: your Crock-Pot.

Most valuable secret. Secret #5: Pour a couple of teaspoons of Kitchen Bouquet on Chuck. You've probably never even heard of Kitchen Bouquet, huh? That's why it's my most valuable secret. You may have to ask your grocer where it is. This is the special ingredient that makes my roast especially great!

Secret #6: If you're not serving mashed potatoes, put small potatoes and carrots in the bottom of your Crock-Pot. Place Chuck on top of the veggies. If you *are* serving mashed potatoes, pour a little water in the bottom of your Crock-Pot and plop Chuck in.

Secret #7: Pour a can of mushroom soup on top of Chuck.

Now that Chuck is secure in his new home, let him cook on low heat all night (about ten hours). When you come home from church, he'll literally fall apart right on your plate. You can make gravy with all the juice from the Crock-Pot. But I'll save that for our next book.

Susie

FROM GOD:

- ❤ "Show hospitality to one another without grumbling" (1 Peter 4:9 ESV).
- ❤ "Share with the Lord's people who are in need. Practice hospitality" (Romans 12:13 NIV).

GO AHEAD—ANSWER:

»—→ What's your favorite Sunday dinner?
»—→ Do you usually eat Sunday dinner alone, with family, or with friends?
»—→ Do you usually eat at home on Sundays or go out to eat?

FROM SUSIE:

A great roast beef dinner is perfect for company. And it doesn't have to be on Sunday! Anytime you make roast beef, it's a special dinner. So go ahead—invite someone over.

FROM KRISTIN:

I really want pot roast now.

46.
Be a blessing to others.

At some point everyone dreams about becoming a super secret agent. (Or was that just me?) You don't have to join an intelligence agency to become a **secret agent of kindness**.

My mom is a great example of distributing kindness. She always made us feel special by surprising us with gifts, notes, and treats.

One day while in college I came out after a long day of classes to find a box of my **favorite candy** and a note sitting on my car windshield. Mom had driven to my school, driven around until she found my car, and left the treat for me. The candy was gone in two minutes, but her **kind gesture** has stayed with me my entire life.

Another time, some girls from my church home group paid me a surprise visit with ice cream and peanut butter cups—all because I'd said at our last meeting that it was my favorite dessert!

Those instances, and countless others, have remained with me as reminders to constantly be on the lookout for chances to distribute RAK (Random Acts of Kindness).

RAK involves looking for ways to **sneak in** little blessings for those around you. Send someone an **encouraging text**. Leave a note in your sibling's lunch box. Bake cookies and put them on your neighbor's porch, ring the doorbell, then **run away**. Do the dishes, even if it's not your turn, and don't expect anything in return. These are just a few of **many ways** you can touch someone.

Here's the **super secret bonus**: doing kind things for others puts you in a good mood, too!

Kristin

• •

FROM GOD:

- ❤ "Love one another with brotherly affection. Outdo one another in showing honor" (Romans 12:10 ESV).
- ❤ "And let us consider how to stir up one another to love and good works" (Hebrews 10:24 ESV).

GO AHEAD—ANSWER:

>—→ Have you been the recipient of Random Acts of Kindness? How'd they make you feel?

>—→ What are some ways God reminds you that He loves you?

>—→ Read Romans 12:10 again. What do you think your home, community, or church would look like if people *actually* tried to outdo one another in showing honor?

FROM KRISTIN:

We generously love others because we recognize that God generously loved us first!

47.
Cast all your cares upon the Lord.

Seriously. Why load yourself down with **worry** when you can give it to God? He actually **wants** your concerns because:

He doesn't have enough to do.

Earthquakes, tornados, and tsunamis have become boring.

He loves you so much that He delights in taking ownership of your burdens.

Good news! Christ not only died for your sins; He also died for your worries.

Which of the following **best** describes how you handle something you're worried about?

Scenario #1: "Okay, class. Put your books away and take out a sheet of paper. This quiz will count for a full weekly grade."

Jessica's heart dropped. She'd forgotten all about the test. Her mouth went dry, and her hands were getting clammy. She felt dizzy. *What am I gonna do?* she thought. *I haven't even read the chapter!*

"Mrs. Wilburton? May I see the nurse? I'm serious. I feel really, really sick."

"God, You know I haven't read the chapter, but I've been listening in class and taking great notes. Please help me calm down and remember what I've learned."

I can't believe I forgot about this! I'm so stupid. I'll never pass. I'll have to cheat off of Brandon.

Scenario #2: The spring dance is only two weeks away. Some of your friends already have dates. You've been crushing on Justin and hoping he'll ask you. He hasn't made a move, though, and you're starting to worry you won't have a date. You:

a. Start acting like you're not interested. "Yeah, I'm not sure I'll be able to go," you tell your friends. "My family's doing some pretty important things that I may have to help with."

b. Begin stalking Justin so everywhere he goes. . .you're just *there*!

c. Pray. "Father, You know how much I want to go to the spring dance with Justin. If it's Your will, please guide him to ask me. If it's not Your will, give me Your peace about it and help me come up with a fun Plan B with other girls who don't have dates."

Can you see how casting all your cares into God's lap actually makes you more confident? Think about it this way: Let's say you're worried about having enough money to participate in the mission trip God has called you to.

You didn't know this, but Donald Trump is your best friend's uncle. And you had no idea that when she invited you to have dinner with her family Saturday evening, he'd be there. Through polite chitchat you talk about the mission trip. Your friend asks how much money you still owe on the trip. After you tell her, Uncle Donald speaks up. "I'll take care of that for you."

"Are you serious, Mr. Trump?"

"Yes, I'm serious. Consider it taken care of."

You leave your friend's house walking pretty tall. Your shoulders are straight. You can't wait to tell your mom. When she says, "Honey, are you sure?" you quickly respond with, "Yes, I'm sure. He gave me his word." You're confident the finances for your trip are covered.

Psalm 50:10 tells us that God owns the cattle on a thousand hills. In other words, He's the richest One in the entire universe. He has waaaaay more moo-lah than Mr. Trump can even think about! If your heavenly Father cares about the lilies of the fields (see Matthew 6:28), won't He take care of **your** needs?

Go ahead. Cast all your cares upon the Lord. And walk in confidence!

Susie

. . . .

FROM GOD:

♥ "Don't worry about anything; instead, pray about everything" (Philippians 4:6 NLT).

♥ "Can all your worries add a single moment to your life?" (Luke 12:25 NLT).

GO AHEAD—ANSWER:

»—→ In what ways does worry most commonly affect you? (Headache, stomach problems, sleeplessness. . .)

»—→ What things do you most commonly worry about?

»—→ Will you give those worries to God right now?

FROM SUSIE:

When we worry about things, it shows we're not trusting God with the problem. When we genuinely give Him our worries, we learn to live freely and lightly!

48.
Get your beauty sleep.

The **best** feeling in the world is waking up in the morning after getting a full night's rest. Just like eating right and exercising, getting sleep is a way of taking care of yourself—it's good stewardship of your body.

Sleep helps you **think clearly**, stay healthy, and focus. It puts you in a **better mood**, gives you energy, and increases your memory. It gives your body time to heal and recharge from the day's activities.

With all those benefits, why wouldn't you try and get to bed early and take advantage of this completely free aptitude booster?

Here are a few tips to help you get some decent shut-eye.

Right before bed _don't_:
- Eat sweets or drink caffeinated beverages.
- Watch scary or intense movies or television shows.
- Drink fourteen cups of water. (Unless you sleep in a bathroom.)
- Exercise. Make sure to exercise, just not right before hitting the hay.
- Start on a project that's due tomorrow. Plan ahead.
- Video-chat with a friend. You'll talk too long.

Right before bed _do_:
- Turn off your computer and phone.
- Drink a small glass of warm milk or cup of decaf tea.
- Create a bedtime routine and stick to it.
- Get everything you need ready for tomorrow.
- Listen to some calming music.
- Read a slow-paced book.

Sweet dreams!

Kristin

• •

FROM GOD:

- ♥ "It is in vain that you rise up early and go late to rest, eating the bread of anxious toil; for he gives to his beloved sleep" (Psalm 127:2 ESV).
- ♥ "If you lie down, you will not be afraid; when you lie down, your sleep will be sweet" (Proverbs 3:24 ESV).

GO AHEAD—ANSWER:

»—→ Do you get enough sleep?
»—→ What happens when you don't get enough rest?
»—→ Do you go to bed early, or do you force yourself to stay awake until
    your eyes can't stay open?

FROM KRISTIN:

I sleep with a notebook beside my bed so if I think of anything funny or that I need to do I can write it down quickly and not lose sleep worrying I'll forget it!

FROM SUSIE:

Sleeping is my spiritual gift. I can sleep anywhere, anytime. In fact, I was asleep the whole time I was working on this book.

49.
Don't drive and text.

Your mother personally asked me to put this in here.

Okay, let's be **honest** for a second. Have you ever been driving and pulled out your phone to text someone?

"It'll be quick," you tell yourself. "Besides, the stuff that happens when people text and drive is rare and won't happen to me."

Stop right there. Put that phone away. **Do *not* text and drive.**

It's **stupid.**

It puts **you** and **other drivers** at risk.

Hear me: you are *not* invincible. As "on top of the world" as you feel, you've the **same chance** of crashing while **texting** as everyone else. And it *does* happen.

This rule also goes for applying makeup, eating, reading, or doing anything that distracts you from the road. If it pulls your eyes off the road, even for a second, put it away!

Instead, put your phone in your purse or backpack, and put *that* in the back-seat. You'll be **less tempted** to pull it out and look at it if it's not right next to you.

I'm going to take this one step further: if you're in the car at all, either as a passenger *or* driver, put away your phone!

Back in my day (I'm officially old now that I've said that) we used to spend time talking to the other people in the car, playing games, joking, and interacting. Riding in the car was time for **bonding** and character building. (Ever had to double buckle for an hour ride to the lake?) It's not a time for isolating yourself.

If you're driving alone, it's a great opportunity to **sing** at the top of your lungs, practice speaking in **various accents**, or simply reflecting. Just be sure to stay focused on what's going on around you.

Kristin

• •

FROM GOD:

- ♥ "The way of a fool is right in his own eyes, but a wise man listens to advice" (Proverbs 12:15 ESV).
- ♥ "A man without self-control is like a city broken into and left without walls" (Proverbs 25:28 ESV).

GO AHEAD—ANSWER:

»——→ Do you text, talk, or do other things while driving that distract you from the road? Why? Can you stop?

»——→ Do you think irresponsibility displeases God? Why or why not?

»——→ Are you addicted to your technology to the point that it's endangering your life?

FROM KRISTIN:

There's enough danger in the world without being reckless. Just put your phone down when you're driving. Do it.

50.
Read good books.

I used to teach creative writing, speech, and drama in a public high school. I remember telling my students, "If you want to be a good writer, read good writing. Saturate yourself with it."

Are you **familiar** with the movie *Finding Forrester?* It's an older movie that came out in 2000 and tells the story of an African-American teen, Jamal Wallace, who was invited into a prestigious **private** high school. By chance, Jamal **befriended** a well-known writer—William Forrester—who had gone into hiding.

Jamal **yearns** to develop his own writing skills, so Mr. Forrester instructs Jamal to copy published pieces of Forrester's own work for a set amount of time each day **before** he attempts to write anything on his own. In this way, Jamal learns to **saturate** his mind with quality writing—picking up the **rhythm**, sentence structure, and verbiage—that soon begin to reflect itself in his own writing.

Reading good books fills your mind with **creativity**, snappy dialogue, exciting adventure, **knowledge**, plot, resolution, and simply great material. Of course, the best book you can read is the Bible. Strive to read it through **once a year**.

But also make a point to read at least two biographies a year. Choose inventors, political figures, and missionaries. **Learn** what they thought while growing up and how they set goals and met them.

Toss in a few good fiction books and study **character development** and how the dialogue transpires. Is it realistic? Does the plot give you something good to talk about with your friends?

Determine to read at least **three** nonfiction spiritual growth books during the year as well. These are books that teach you how to grow spiritually and help you **deepen** your faith.

I encourage EVERYONE to read *The Heavenly Man: The Remarkable True Story of Chinese Christian Brother Yun*, *Passport through Darkness*, *Hinds' Feet on High Places*, *Pilgrim's Progress*, *Radical*, *Crazy Love*, and *The Case for Christ*.

Susie

• •

FROM GOD:

- ❤ "Set your minds on things above, not on earthly things" (Colossians 3:2 NIV).
- ❤ "Finally, brothers and sisters, whatever is true, whatever is noble, whatever is right, whatever is pure, whatever is lovely, whatever is admirable—if anything is excellent or praiseworthy—think about such things" (Philippians 4:8 NIV).

GO AHEAD—ANSWER:

»⟶ What's the most recent book you've read? Was it your choice, or was it an assignment?

»⟶ How can reading good books help you develop into a more well-rounded person?

»⟶ Will you commit to reading one of the books listed above in the next few weeks?

FROM SUSIE:

I've never regretted reading a good book!

51.
Be "others centered."

Maybe you've heard the saying about joy:

JOY = Jesus (first), Others (second), Yourself (last).

It's true! As you focus on Jesus, others, and yourself in this specific order, you **really do** experience true joy!

Don't wait until you're out of college to adapt this lifestyle. **Start right now!** How can you become "others centered"? What can you do to put the needs of others before yourself?

1. Start with **prayer**. Ask God to help you develop a **heart** for others. As you watch the news and read the paper, be praying for those in your community who are hurting.

2. Ask your **pastor** if your church is involved in any kind of social needs program. Many churches offer a food pantry, classes for the disabled, recovery groups—services you may not be aware of that are already happening. **Find out** what your church is doing so you won't unnecessarily try to duplicate the same **ministry**.

3. Ask about needs in your **church**. Are there some older people who would love for you to get their groceries for them? Someone who needs her lawn mowed but doesn't have a mower and can't afford to pay anyone? I spoke in a church that offered a monthly oil change for single women. On the first Saturday of each month, a woman could bring her car to the church parking lot for a free oil change. This was an amazing gift! And imagine their **surprise** as the youth group volunteered to wash their cars after the oil change!

4. Reach out to the needs of your **community** after you've exhausted the needs in your church. Serve at a soup kitchen, volunteer at an assisted living or nursing home. Many of the patients have children who live in another state, and unfortunately, they don't get any visitors. Paint their nails, comb their hair, or **volunteer** to read the Bible to them.

5. Engage yourself in a variety of service acts: fold bulletins at your church, help with a local theater production, help your **neighbor** with her kids.

You'll not only *feel* good about placing the needs of others before yourself, you'll be developing character along the way!

Susie

FROM GOD:

❤ "Do not forget to show hospitality to strangers, for by so doing some people have shown hospitality to angels without knowing it" (Hebrews 13:2 NIV).

❤ "Each of you should use whatever gift you have received to serve others, as faithful stewards of God's grace in its various forms" (1 Peter 4:10 NIV).

GO AHEAD—ANSWER:

»—→ Describe someone you know who puts Jesus first, others second, and herself last. What stands out about her life?

»—→ What changes would you need to make in order to live the JOY lifestyle?

»—→ Will you ask Christ to reshape your heart toward others?

FROM SUSIE:

People love to be around someone who genuinely cares about their needs. As you allow God to turn your heart toward others, you'll naturally become more aware of the numerous careers available in serving others. Who knows? God may lead you into a career of exciting service!

FROM KRISTIN:

The best place to start learning how to be "others centered" is in your home! Start putting your family members above yourself. It's tough sometimes, but well worth the effort!

52.
Don't make big decisions when you're tired or upset.

If you haven't figured it out already, your mind reacts **a little differently** when you're tired, **under stress**, or at particular times of the month. (That's the only time we'll mention this in the whole book. Promise!)

During those times it's **easy** to say or do things that you might regret later when you're thinking a bit more rationally.

When tired, stressed, or upset, **avoid the following**:

- Making big decisions. **Don't** decide to give the teacher a piece of your mind, quit school, or get a drastic haircut while running on three hours of sleep.
- Sending **confrontational** texts or e-mails. You'll probably **regret** most of what you say.
- Posting on **Facebook**. Your status *will* be **whiny and petty**.
- Going shopping. You'll spend too much **money**.
- Eating at a **buffet**. It's debatable whether buffets are *ever* a good idea, but they're **most definitely** a bad idea when stressed or tired. You'll end up eating three bowls of clam chowder, six rolls, and half a pound of pepperonis from the salad bar. (I may or may not be writing this from experience.)
- Spending **too much time** on social media. It's easy to get jealous and upset by other people's perfectly portrayed lives when you're tired or upset.

Instead, try **any of the following**:

- Picking up a **good book**.
- Spending some time **praying**, memorizing scripture, and reading the Bible.
- Send a text to a mentor or trusted friend and ask her to pray **for** you or **with** you.
- Take a nap or get a good night's sleep. Chances are, whatever's plaguing you won't seem as bad after you sleep. At the very least, you'll have a clear head when trying to figure it out!
- Send an **encouraging** message or text to a friend. Doing something nice for someone else is often a fast way to turn your mood around!

- Remind yourself this hardship will end and that the Lord is walking beside you, during both big and little trials!

Kristin

• •

FROM GOD:

💙 "In your anger do not sin" (Ephesians 4:26 NIV).

💙 "Be sober-minded; be watchful. Your adversary the devil prowls around like a roaring lion, seeking someone to devour" (1 Peter 5:8 ESV).

GO AHEAD—ANSWER:

»—→ How do you act toward others when you're tired or stressed? Be honest! Do you use your mood as an "excuse" for acting that way?

»—→ How can you keep yourself from sinning when you're tired, upset, or under stress?

»—→ Pray right now that God will give you wisdom and a clear head, even when you don't "feel" like being calm and rational.

FROM KRISTIN:

Whenever you're tempted to make a rash decision that will have serious repercussions, set a timer for twenty-four hours. When the timer goes off, reconsider and see if you still think it's a good idea.

The greatest confidence booster in the world is allowing God to help you lead someone to Christ.

There are a **variety** of ways to share your faith. But the two most common are friendship evangelism and straight evangelism. Let's chat about **straight evangelism** first.

This means you don't have a close relationship with the listener. When you hear a speaker at a crusade or rally, he has a **temporary** relationship with his audience, but he's **not** someone you've actually established anything **long-term** with. When he shares the gospel with the crowd, it's evangelism **straight-up**.

When you participate on a mission trip and share the gospel door-to-door, on street corners, or through a drama, you're doing so without having a relationship with your audience. This is an effective means of evangelism, and God certainly uses it to bring people to Him. The **advantage** is that it doesn't require much prep time. The **disadvantage** is that unless there's follow-up, some of the new Christians may never learn how to grow spiritually.

Friendship evangelism is **time intensive**. After you've established a relationship with someone, you begin sharing the difference Christ has made in your life. **Gradually**, you begin to ask your friend if you can pray for her, you invite her to church, and you end up **leading** her to Christ.

This, too, is a **powerful** means of sharing the gospel! God uses Christians daily to build His kingdom by sharing their faith with friends, family members, and coworkers.

The **advantage** is that because you have a relationship with this person, he or she is more likely to get involved in your church and a Bible study because you're there to **nurture** the growth. The **disadvantage** is simply that it's a slower process.

I don't really think God favors one method over another. What I *do* know is that when He **nudges** us to share our faith, we need to obey. Sometimes He'll nudge you to use straight evangelism (with the person next to you on an **airplane**) and other times He'll nudge you to ask your friend if she's thought about where she'll spend **eternity**.

But one thing is for certain: when you DO lead someone to Christ, it's an **amazing** experience! Wow. **Be ready.**

Susie

FROM GOD:

- ❤ "Therefore go and make disciples of all nations, baptizing them in the name of the Father and of the Son and of the Holy Spirit, and teaching them to obey everything I have commanded you" (Matthew 28:19–20 NIV).
- ❤ "Then Peter stepped forward with the eleven apostles, and shouted to the crowd. 'Listen all of you, visitors and residents of Jerusalem alike! . . . In the last days, God said, "I will pour out my Holy Spirit upon all mankind, and your sons and daughters shall prophesy, and your young men shall see visions, and your old men dream dreams:" ' " (Acts 2:14, 17 TLB).

GO AHEAD—ANSWER:

- »⟶ What's the biggest hindrance you face in sharing your faith?
- »⟶ Where would you be spending eternity if someone hadn't shared the gospel with you? Ask God to give you a genuine burden for those who don't have a relationship with Him.
- »⟶ Pray every morning this week that God will give you an opportunity to share your faith during the day. Then watch expectantly for Him to miraculously open the door!

FROM SUSIE:

The greatest honor I've ever experienced is the privilege of leading someone into a personal relationship with Jesus Christ. To know that this specific person will be in heaven forever simply because I shared my faith. . .is mind-boggling!

54.
Make a list.

Why is this important? Because it helps you **remember** what you're supposed to do. You can even get a free app for your phone that allows you to make your list on your phone. I've made lists on the back of envelopes, **napkins**, paper towels, cardboard, gum wrappers, calendars—it's not important *where* you make your list—just make one.

Here's a **peek** at my list from last week: Take Obie and Amos to the dog park, buy more orange juice, lunch with Steph, buy **lime-green** shoelaces (Amos chewed up my others), haircut, Obie and Amos to the groomer's, take out trash, remove lint from dryer, watch **OKC Thunder basketball** game with Deb and Rhonda, get chips and pie and Coke and salsa and pizza for game-watching, finish writing book with Kristin.

See, if I hadn't made this list, I would've forgotten to finish writing **this book**! Your list might look something like this:

Find shoes, finish homework, **wash dishes for Mom**, read Susie and Kristin's book, send Susie and Kristin a note telling them how much you love the book and give them ideas for their next one, clean the litter box, hug parents.

See, if you didn't have the above list, you might have forgotten to **hug** your mom and dad! By putting it on a list, however, it now becomes something you do and then get to check off. You become **intentional** about it! It prevents laziness, and it provides direction and organization for your day.

Susie

• •

FROM GOD:

- ♥ "Some men are so lazy they won't even feed themselves!" (Proverbs 19:2 TLB).
- ♥ "God delights in those who keep their promises and abhors those who don't" (Proverbs 12:22 TLB).

GO AHEAD—ANSWER:

»——→ Identify something really important that you forgot to do. If you'd put it on a list or written yourself a note, would you have had a better chance of remembering?

»——→ Challenge yourself to make a list for each day of the week for two weeks. Some lists can just be for fun, such as: list everything you can think of that's orange. At the end of two weeks, tell someone what kind of difference it has made for you.

»——→ A list also works great for prayer requests. Don't tell someone you'll pray for her if you'll probably forget. Write it down. Make a list of things to pray for and record the date when God answers those prayers.

FROM SUSIE:

#54 Done. Ahhh. That felt great!

55.

Help keep "creepsters" away by disabling all location information on your social media.

Here's the deal: We live in an age where you can announce to everyone every-where **what** you're doing, **where** you're going, **when** you'll be there, and **who** you'll be with. It's an open invitation for stalkers and uninvited people to crash your life.

You may be saying to yourself, "That couldn't happen to me" or "Who'd care enough about my life, other than my friends, to do that?"

Hopefully you're right, but I know several cases where girls posted too much personal information online and began getting nasty e-mails, phone calls, and texts from strangers who knew a lot about them and had developed disturbing infatuations. It's scary.

Considering **you have control** over the information you put out, doesn't it seem **wise** to eliminate this potential threat as much as possible?

Be **very selective** about what you post.

Don't put your exact city or town in your location. Instead, put a broader, larger city close to where you live.

Don't post exactly when you'll be somewhere. Post afterward, once you've already left. Be general instead of specific.

Don't *friend* or allow anyone to *follow* you if you don't know him or her.

Don't post photos with your address, street, or school name on the back-ground.

It's easy to get **sloppy** and **relaxed** on these measures, so have a parent, friend, or mentor help monitor what you put up so you can keep private informa-tion private!

Kristin

FROM GOD:

- ❤ "Behold, I am sending you out as sheep in the midst of wolves, so be wise as serpents and innocent as doves" (Matthew 10:16 ESV).
- ❤ "In peace I will both lie down and sleep; for you alone, O LORD, make me dwell in safety" (Psalm 4:8 ESV).

GO AHEAD—ANSWER:

»—→ Have you become too free with the information you share about yourself?

»—→ We're to be wise as serpents, but innocent as doves. How can we be "wise as serpents" in the way we handle our personal information online?

»—→ Go look over your information now and see if there's anything that reveals too much.

FROM KRISTIN:

There's no need to live in fear of people stalking your every move, but you also want to be careful and make sure you don't unknowingly put yourself in harm's way!

56.
Seek after the Lord with all your heart, mind, and soul.

Learn about who God is. Ask the tough questions, and determine to find the answers.

Someone once asked Jesus what the greatest command was, and Jesus replied, "Love the Lord your God with all your heart and with all your soul and with all your mind" (Matthew 22:37 NIV).

To **love** God requires **knowing** Him. And knowing Him involves **seeking** Him. It's cyclical. The more we seek Him, the more we know Him. The more we know Him, the more we love Him. The more we love Him, the more we seek Him. The more we seek Him, the more we know Him. . . .

So how **can** you seek God with all your **heart**, mind, and soul? Let's take a peek at what the heart, mind, and soul involve. The **heart** is the wellspring of your **emotions**. So to seek God emotionally means that you'll love Him, talk with Him, and share your entire being with Him. When you give Him your heart, you're trusting Him emotionally. You're allowing Him to **guard** your heart and to write your love story. It means you'll allow Him to direct your relationships.

Your mind houses your **intellect**. To seek God with your mind means that you'll allow yourself to be challenged intellectually by His Word. You'll develop a desire to **study** scripture, memorize it, and appreciate the doctrine and **theology** of your faith. Visit your local Christian bookstore for a variety of books on apologetics that can help deepen your **spiritual intellect**.

To seek God with your **soul** is to seek Him with everything you are. Your gifts and creativity are **stored** in your soul. As you seek God with **passion** in worship and praise, you're seeking Him with your soul—with your entire being.

The bottom line? To seek God with all your heart, mind, and soul means to dive **100 percent** into a relationship with Him and to go after it with gusto! Give Him all you are, all you have, and even commit your **future** to Him. And as you do this, you'll automatically fall in love with God in a deep way!

Susie

• •

FROM GOD:

♥ "So this is my prayer: that your love will flourish and that you will not only love much but well. Learn to love appropriately. You need to use your head and test your feelings so that your love is sincere and intelligent, not sentimental gush" (Philippians 1:9–10 MSG).

♥ "Early in the morning before the sun is up, I am praying and pointing out how much I trust in you. I stay awake through the night to think about your promises" (Psalm 119:147–148 TLB).

GO AHEAD—ANSWER:

»—→ What difference do you hope to see God make in your relationships when you seek Him with all your heart?

»—→ How will your reading, TV, and movie selections change when you seek God with all your mind?

»—→ How will your music choices be affected when you seek God with all your soul?

FROM SUSIE:

Years ago I made this commitment to God: "Lord, anything. . .anytime. . .anywhere. I'm Yours, Father." I've never second-guessed it. He is always faithful!

57.

Give people the benefit of the doubt.

Not giving the benefit of the doubt really only hurts you.

It's not only **embarrassing** to jump to conclusions and assume the worst in someone; it also makes you look **bad**. For example, who looks worse in the following scenarios?

YOU: Well, I'm still waiting on the e-mail you promised three days ago.

HANNAH: I sent it three days ago. Have you checked your spam? Maybe it went in there by mistake.

YOU: Oh. Yeah, here it is. Sorry.

SIMON: Hi! Sorry I'm late.

YOU: This is really frustrating! It seems as though you're *always* late.

SIMON: I passed a wreck on the way here and saw a little girl and her mom crying by the side of the road as they watched the wrecker tow away their car. I happened to notice a teddy bear that had been thrown several feet from the wreck, so I stopped and got it for the little girl. She was so happy to get it back.

YOU: Oh. Well, that was nice of you. I'm sorry.

YOU: Abby, what are you doing here at the coffee shop? I thought you had your job interview this morning. Oh no! You slept through it, didn't you?

Abby: Not at all. They called me and postponed it until next week.

YOU: Oh. Yeah, that makes sense.

In each of the above situations, you would have actually come out on **top** if you'd given your friend the **benefit** of the doubt. Doing so helps kindness take **root** and grow strong in our lives. As Christians, we *want* the fruit of the Spirit (love, joy, peace, patience, kindness, goodness, self-control, gentleness, faithfulness—see Galatians 5:22–23) to **manifest** itself through our actions and reactions.

What can you use as a **reminder** not to jump to conclusions? Biting your tongue before you lash out? Wearing a rubber band on your wrist and snapping yourself before saying something? Praying before the confrontation? Do **whatever it takes** to keep yourself from jumping to conclusions. Giving someone the benefit of the doubt always makes you look good. . .even if the other person is wrong.

Susie

FROM GOD:

- ❤ "Understand this, my dear brothers and sisters: You must all be quick to listen, slow to speak, and slow to get angry" (James 1:19 NLT).
- ❤ "Take tender care of those who are weak. Be patient with everyone" (1 Thessalonians 5:14 NLT).

GO AHEAD—ANSWER:

»— How does it make you feel when someone gives you the benefit of the doubt?

»— Describe a time you gave someone the benefit of the doubt. Did it strengthen your relationship with that person?

»— Why do we sometimes jump to conclusions instead of giving someone the benefit of the doubt?

FROM SUSIE:

When someone gives me the benefit of the doubt, it automatically makes me want to be a better friend, work harder, and respect that person more.

58.
Don't keep mean friends.

Do your friends constantly **make fun** of you in a way that targets your imperfections or weaknesses?

Do your friends **mock** your suggestions, hobbies, and interests?

Do they **gossip** constantly?

Do they give you a **hard time** if you refuse to participate in sinful activities?

Do they **get mad** if you confront them about wrongdoings?

Even good friends have bad days, but if the people you're hanging out with fit any of the above categories, they're **mean friends**. It's better to be **alone** than around **mean**, foolish people.

"Whoever walks with the wise becomes wise, but the companion of fools will suffer harm" (Proverbs 13:20 ESV).

If you keep **hanging** around mean fools, eventually you'll **get hurt**. In addition, you'll **probably** adopt some of their bad behavior and turn around and **hurt others**. Instead, surround yourself with people who **love God** and **love you** for who you are.

You can still be loving and civil to mean people, but it's best to put distance between you and them. Life throws **enough** situations where you'll *have* to be around mean people without *voluntarily* spending more time with them.

Good friends are rare. They're a **gift** from God. One kind, wise, loyal friend is better than forty lukewarm buddies. **Treasure** these relationships.

Always remember, the **greatest companion** you'll ever have is Jesus. Would even your best friend sacrifice her life to pay your debt? **Jesus did.**

Kristin

• •

FROM GOD:

♥ "Do not make friends with a hot-tempered person, do not associate with one easily angered, or you may learn their ways and get yourself ensnared" (Proverbs 22:24–25 NIV).

♥ "The righteous choose their friends carefully, but the way of the wicked leads them astray" (Proverb 12:26 NIV).

GO AHEAD—ANSWER:

»→ Have you had mean friends? Do you still have them?

»→ Why does the Bible tell us not to associate with hot-tempered people? What are the consequences of spending too much time with mean, catty, or angry people?

»→ Take a moment to thank God for the good friendships in your life. Send an encouraging text to a good friend today!

FROM KRISTIN:

Everyone has times when they feel alone. Ask God to bring you meaningful friendships that will last forever!

59.
Get a piggy bank.

A few years ago, I got a **piggy bank** and took it to work and put it in my friend's office. "Let's just put whatever we can in here, whenever either of us have some extra money, and when we have enough, let's go somewhere fun!" I said.

She agreed and named the pig **Portly**. He started getting full. In fact, we went to New York and saw a Broadway play. "Thank you, Portly!"

You'll be **surprised** at how fast your loose change and dollars can add up (see tip #100). You may even be able to take your family on a cool vacation.

Or it could be that you'll use your **piggy savings** to do something for someone else. You could donate your money to Voice of the Martyrs (a Christian ministry to help persecuted Christians) or to help stop human trafficking (A21 is a great ministry that's involved in rescuing girls) or even to a special program your church is involved in.

Start filling your piggy!

Susie

• •

FROM GOD:

- ♥ "I, wisdom, dwell with prudence, and I find knowledge and discretion" (Proverbs 8:12 ESV).
- ♥ "The point is this: whoever sows sparingly will also reap sparingly, and whoever sows bountifully will also reap bountifully" (2 Corinthians 9:6 ESV).

GO AHEAD—ANSWER:

»→ What's the most money you've saved at one time?
»→ Were you saving it for something specific? What did you end up doing with it?
»→ What would you need to do less of in order to save more money?

FROM SUSIE:

I'm an OKC Thunder basketball fan! I now have an OKC Thunder piggy bank that I'm working on filling.

60.
Keep a prayer journal.

Maybe you're already doing this. If not, **now** is a great time to start. Get a cool notebook—if you're doing it by hand. Or decide which fun font you're going to use—if you're doing it on the computer. Designate one section **Prayer Requests** and another section **Answers to Prayer**.

You guessed it. Fill the section of requests with personal prayer requests as well as things you can **pray** about for your family and friends. If you want to be really organized, you can create different sections for family, friends, personal, world, city, school, etc.

When God answers your prayers, record the **answer** and the date. *Why is this important?* So during the times your faith is weak and you're wondering if God is going to answer your prayer, you can look back at the answers He has already given you. It's a surefire faith booster!

Prayer is *really* important. Do you know that your prayers are so important to God that He **saves** each one? (See Revelation 8:3.) Think about it: Every single prayer you have ever prayed—and every prayer you'll pray in the future—will be **saved** by God. Prayers filled with anger, love, gratitude, confusion, fear. He collects them all. *Why?* Because He loves you. He cherishes everything you give Him—especially your prayers.

How **full** will your prayer file be? I hope it's full and overflowing! I hope you're sending up prayers full of questions, confusion, and fear. But I also hope you're praying with gratitude, honor, and love. I hope your prayer file is full of all kinds of prayers. God **loves** it when you pray!

And by the way. . .God *always* answers your prayers! He may not answer them in your timing. His timing and our timing are way different! We're told in 2 Peter 3:8 that a thousand years to us can be just like one day to Him.

Sometimes God answers our prayers with a hearty "Yes!" Sometimes He says, "No." And other times He says, "Not yet." But He **always** answers!

Susie

FROM GOD:

- ❤ "And call on me in the day of trouble; I will deliver you, and you will honor me" (Psalm 50:15 NIV).
- ❤ "Let us come before him with thanksgiving and extol him with music and song" (Psalm 95:2 NIV).

GO AHEAD—ANSWER:

- »—→ Describe the last time God answered one of your prayers.
- »—→ Why is it important to pray?
- »—→ If you don't have a consistent prayer life, commit now to praying every day. Even if it's just short little sentence prayers that you "shoot up" to God, do it daily.

FROM SUSIE:

I begin praying for my family and myself before I even get out of bed in the morning. Then I continue to pray throughout the day. Sometimes it's simply a casual one-sentence prayer: "Thanks for that fun surprise, God!" to a prayer of searching filled with tears or hurt. And sometimes it's just an "I love You, Jesus!"

61.
Be willing to adjust your expectations.

Things in life won't always work out like you're expecting.

Sometimes we put an incredible amount of time and energy into something, only to have it turn out **completely different** than we expected.

You may work **really hard** on a project, only to get a D.

Your family may plan an *awesome* vacation to your dream destination, but a hurricane requires all flights to cancel and instead of riding rides or relaxing on the beach you sit in the airport for three days.

Everyone tells you you're a shoo-in for the lead part in the school play, but instead you get cast as a singing tree. (You can bark out the notes. Get it?)

It's easy to get upset, angry, or feel sorry for yourself when things don't go the way you expect. But all of those reactions reveal you **lack trust** in God.

Thwarted plans remind us that **we are not in control**. No matter how disappointing or discouraging an outcome, though, God works **all things** together for the good of those who love Him. (See Romans 8:28.)

God uses **unexpected situations** to do big things. He may use your small part in the play to **refine** your character and teach you teamwork. He may use a delayed flight to give you an opportunity to **witness** to someone. Perhaps you won't see what He has in mind immediately, or ever, but you **can rest knowing** your situation hasn't escaped His tender, loving hand.

Learning to adjust expectations now prepares you for life's larger disappointments.

Your dream college may turn you down. **Marriage** may not be a perfect fairy tale. You may stay single a **long time** or **forever**.

Take every situation, big or small, and run it through the following filter: **What attitude and/or action will glorify God in this moment?**

Next time something unexpected happens, take a moment to thank God for being with you in the situation. Next, pray for **grace** to handle it. It's hard to **muster up praise** when your car breaks down or when you're sick and missing work and bills need to be paid, but **rejoicing** in the Lord is the best course of action!

Kristin

FROM GOD:

- ❤ "In their hearts humans plan their course, but the LORD establishes their steps" (Proverbs 16:9 NIV).
- ❤ "Come now, you who say, 'Today or tomorrow we will go into such and such a town and spend a year there and trade and make a profit'—yet you do not know what tomorrow will bring" (James 4:13–14 ESV).

GO AHEAD—ANSWER:

- »→ What are some good things that can come out of an inconvenient situation?
- »→ Why do you think God puts us through these unexpected circumstances?
- »→ How is your attitude typically when you feel like you're losing control?

FROM KRISTIN:

No matter how many times I read the Lord's Prayer, it still says "Thy will be done" not "my will be done." We should praise God for that because His will is so much better!

62.
Introduce yourself to new people.

I've talked to many people over the years who feel insecure, **unwelcome**, or anxious in large or unfamiliar groups. If *you* feel this way, it's **safe to assume** a few *others* feel this way.

Group settings can be really lonely if you don't know anyone. There's a little trick, though, that'll help you make friends in any situation. Want to learn it? Don't worry. It's **super** easy.

Next time you're with a group of strangers, look around and find someone you've never met. Go up to them, **smile**, and say, "Hi, my name is _____. What's your name?" **Follow it up** with a few questions related to where you are. If you're at church, **ask** how long they've attended. If you're at a party, **ask** how they know the host. If you're at a school event, **ask** what classes they're in.

Sometimes you have to take the first step out of your shell.

"In the morning sow your seed, and at evening withhold not your hand, for you do not know which will prosper, this or that, or whether both alike will be good" (Ecclesiastes 11:6 ESV).

Don't get discouraged if your introductions don't instantly lead to dozens of "bosom buddies." (Do you know which classic book coined the term "bosom buddies"?) Simply **sow seeds of friendship**, and eventually you will reap!

Making friends is a perk of reaching out, but it's ultimately about something bigger. It's about **obeying** Christ's instruction to put others first. Instead of creating an elaborate social circle for *you*, focus on making sure *others* feel included. Treat *them* as you would like to be treated: **like someone who is welcome and belongs.**

Kristin

• •

FROM GOD:

❤ "Whoever brings blessing will be enriched, and one who waters will himself be watered" (Proverbs 11:25 ESV).

❤ "So in everything, do to others what you would have them do to you, for this sums up the Law and the Prophets" (Matthew 7:12 NIV).

GO AHEAD—ANSWER:

»——→ Are you an introvert or extrovert? Is it easy for you to talk to strangers? What keeps you from reaching out to new people?

»——→ How did Jesus act toward those outside His immediate circle? What can we pull from that on how to treat those outside our circle?

»——→ Pray that God gives you a sensitive heart to reach out to those who are new, alone, or have trouble fitting in.

FROM KRISTIN:

Even if you have a lot of friends, always be on the lookout for new people who may not know anyone. Don't get so caught up in your current social circle that you forget to include others!

63.
Make your bed.

You're probably asking, "What's the big deal?" Actually it's not a *big* deal, but it *is* important. When you **make** your bed, it's **proof** that you actually had time to make it! That means you've also had time to look your **best** and to feel "put together" before leaving the house.

When you have your act together, you'll **naturally** act and react better in relationships, friendships, and to authorities. You'll also feel more **confident** in yourself. It's amazing how a simple thing like taking the time to **make your bed** can actually make your entire day seem smoother.

I have to be honest: there are days I **don't** make my bed. (Please don't tell anyone. This is just between us.) And sure enough—on those days—I just never feel really together. I feel like I'm **halfway** dressed—just not really ready to meet the day and the challenges I know I'll face.

Making your bed isn't a magic **formula** for success. But it makes you *feel* better about yourself. You seem more organized. Better equipped to handle the **stuff** life will toss your way. And again, when you feel good about yourself, you're more **confident**.

There's a **secret** to making your bed. If you allow yourself to get in the habit of pushing the **snooze button** on your alarm, you won't have time to make your bed. So the secret is disciplining yourself to get up **exactly** when the alarm goes off. To do this, you have to **plan** to do it! Go to bed early enough tonight that you can realistically make yourself get up tomorrow morning without pushing the snooze button.

When you've learned this **secret**, you'll be amazed at the positive way this will affect other areas in your life! Making your bed also adds a nice "closure" element to your life before you leave the house and dive into your day. It's something you can cross off your "to-do list." (See Tip #54.)

Besides beginning your day with things in order, making your bed provides one more **positive** element. It feels great to climb into a cozy bed that's made up and neat instead of fighting your way across a lump of crumpled sheets and blankets.

Susie

FROM GOD:

- ❤ "For though I am absent from you in body, I am present with you in spirit and delight to see how disciplined you are and how firm your faith in Christ is" (Colossians 2:5 NIV).
- ❤ "But everything should be done in a fitting and orderly way" (1 Corinthians 14:40 NIV).

GO AHEAD—ANSWER:

»——→ How much time would it take for you to make your bed each morning? Will you start doing it?

»——→ How many times do you usually hit the snooze button before getting up? Will you implement a plan to get up when the alarm goes off?

»——→ Describe the difference you'd notice in your day if you began it feeling confident and put together.

FROM SUSIE:

I have to stop writing now and go make my bed!

64.

Keep televisions and computers out of your room.

This is to protect **yourself**!

You already know that Satan hates your guts and will do anything to trip you. That's putting it nicely. He's truly out to kill you! He delights in your failure. He laughs at your mistakes. Each time you're a little down on yourself, he dances.

He can make you doubt your self-worth, tempt you in ways you think you can't escape, torment you, oppress you, afflict you, and trick you. He's crafty, cunning, evil, despicable, vile, poisonous, and wicked. He is hatred personified. There is **nothing** good about him. **Nothing** of redemptive value. And because he's going down forever, he wants to take you with him!

You don't have to think too much to imagine what he can do with a student, a computer, and a room with no adult supervision. Be wise. Think smart. Don't fall for it.

Move your computer into a public area of the house, such as a corner of the living room, the kitchen, or anywhere there will be lots of traffic. Also talk with your parents about your desire to live a holy life. Tell them about filters, etc., that work to keep pornography away from your Internet searches. It may seem like a hassle now, but it will be much more of a hassle later when you've seen images you can't get out of your mind!

Never look at **anything** on the computer you wouldn't look at with Christ sitting next to you. He is. . .you know. Sitting next to you.

Susie

• •

FROM GOD:

- ♥ "For God has not called us to be dirty-minded and full of lust, but to be holy and clean" (1 Thessalonians 4:7 TLB).
- ♥ "For God wants you to be holy and pure and to keep clear of all sexual sin. . ." (1 Thessalonians 4:4 TLB).

GO AHEAD—ANSWER:

»—→ What has surprised you most popping up on your computer that you hadn't expected?

»—→ What can you do to live a holy life while saturated in a media-savvy world?

»—→ Who can you ask to hold you accountable about what you do on the computer?

FROM SUSIE:

I travel and speak about forty weeks/weekends out of the year. With this much travel, I have to keep my guard up regarding TV. The computer really isn't a temptation to me—it's the TV. I have to be very careful about channel surfing and what I choose to watch. I don't want to hurt my heavenly Father. I'm glad I have people who pray for me as I travel. Be willing to do whatever it takes to guard yourself from evil!

65

Think really, really hard before you get a tattoo or seventeen facial piercings.

Do you have the deep desire to get a tattoo or tons of facial piercings? If so, **why?** If you answer **"because they're cool"** or something similar, I will physically pop out of the pages of this book and shake you by the shoulders. **Think!**

You belong to Christ and should honor Him in all you do. This includes thinking really, **really** hard before doing something permanent or extreme to your body.

Let's look at what the Bible says about it.

"You shall not make any cuts on your body for the dead or tattoo yourselves: I am the LORD" (Leviticus 19:28 ESV).

This was a law given to the Old Testament Israelites. They were required to obey it. **We're no longer under the old law** because Jesus came and fulfilled it, but let's look at why God gave them this law. He wanted them to be **set apart.** The cultures and tribes around them were obviously cutting themselves as a tribute to the dead and tattooing themselves, perhaps as a way of worshiping false gods. God didn't want **His people** being associated in any way with pagan customs.

God wanted His people to look different.

This hasn't changed. God still wants His people to stand out. He wants us to stand out in a specific way, though. He wants us to focus **inward**, not outward. Everything about us, including how we dress, **what we say**, how we spend our money, and **what we do to our bodies** reflects what Christ has done for us.

While tattoos and facial piercings may **no longer** be biblically forbidden, in many cultures they represent an attitude of rebellion or an association with certain non-Christian groups.

Think about the sign tattoos send in your culture. Do they say, **"I've been bought and paid for by Christ,"** or do they say, **"I'm a rebel who's living for me"?** Think about it.

" 'All things are lawful,' but not all things are helpful. 'All things are lawful,' but not all things build up" (1 Corinthians 10:23 ESV).

Even though getting a tattoo won't prevent you from getting into heaven, or even prevent your growth as a Christian, it could hinder your witness as a Christian.

What if I want to get a verse or cross tattooed? It could open the door to witness to someone!

It could. God can use **anything** to get His Word out. He used a donkey. He could use your tattoo. God brings good out of our mistakes. That's not a **good enough reason** to do something unwise, though.

Finally, tattoos are **permanent**. What seems beautiful now may not look so great after thirty years of gravity and sun exposure. That verse you had tattooed may just wind up being **a long black smudge**. People **may not** ask about the verse anymore. Instead they may ask how you hurt your arm.

If you really, really want one, **wait at least a year**. Think about it, weigh the costs (and not just financial), and decide. It could be that you truly want to commemorate a particularly meaningful verse (still. . .try sewing it onto a hand towel or framing it!). Or maybe tattoos are so normal in your culture they've lost the "rebel" stigma generally attached to them.

Ask your parents their thoughts. If they're completely against it, **honor them** and don't get it. **A little bit of ink or an extra piercing isn't worth causing a family rift.** If you want to prove you're mature enough to get one, show them by respecting their wishes and not getting one.

Finally, ask someone a few decades older who's been where you are their thoughts. **Glean wisdom from their hindsight.**

Kristin

• •

FROM GOD:

♥ "Or do you not know that your body is a temple of the Holy Spirit within you, whom you have from God? You are not your own, for you were bought with a price. So glorify God in your body" (1 Corinthians 6:19–20 ESV).

♥ "And try to discern what is pleasing to the Lord" (Ephesians 5:10 ESV).

GO AHEAD–ANSWER:

»——→ Why does God call us to be different? In what ways should our lives look different as believers?

»——→ Do you think it's old-fashioned and legalistic to discourage or forbid tattoos and facial piercings? Why or why not?

»——→ When dealing with "gray areas" in the Bible, do you think it's better to err on the side of being safe?

FROM KRISTIN:

Always check, double-check, and then triple-check your motives!

66.
Identify and eliminate any idols in your life.

The Old Testament is full of stories of people who worshipped idols—man-made statues—instead of God. Because of that, many of us tend to think of idols as a statue. One of the most popular idols in the Old Testament was Baal. . .again, a man-made statue. We still have idols in the form of statues today. For example, the Buddha figure is an idol to Buddhists.

But an idol is more than a statue! It's anything that's AS important as God or anything that's MORE important than God.

For example, if your boyfriend is as important to you as God is, he's an idol.

Love your car, your job, your sport as much as God? If so, they've become idols to you.

The Old Testament book of Deuteronomy reveals God directing His people in chapter 3 to destroy the ungodly things. In other words, He's calling for a holy destruction. In Deuteronomy 3:1–11 God tells His people to destroy a heathen city, an ungodly army, and a wicked king (King Og).

We get a fascinating piece of information in Deuteronomy 3:11. We're given a description of King Og's bed! "His bed was made of iron and was more than thirteen feet long and six feet wide" (NLT).

That's a honkin' big bed! Why do we have these details? Do we really care about the size of wicked King Og's bed?

I think God let us in on this detail because He wants us to know that the quality of your stuff doesn't matter to Him. If it's keeping you from passionately, fervently knowing Him in all His fullness, it needs to be destroyed. Eliminated. Smashed. Bon voyaged.

God is calling you to know Him in His fullness. But that can't happen if there's an idol in your life. And the only one who can destroy the idol. . .is you! He will give you the strength you need, but you have to be the one to destroy it.

And here's a surefire plan to make sure you don't bring back the idols into your life: pray Psalm 139:23–24 every single day and obey God. If you do this—and mean it—you can't help but grow closer to Him!

Susie

· ·

FROM GOD:

- ❤ "Do not turn to idols or make metal gods for yourselves. I am the LORD your God" (Leviticus 19:4 NIV).
- ❤ "Do not make any idols" (Exodus 34:17 NIV).

GO AHEAD—ANSWER:

- »⟶ Ask God right now to bring to your mind anything in your life that has become too important to you.
- »⟶ When God brings something or someone to your attention, ask His forgiveness and surrender that area of your life to Him.
- »⟶ Will you commit to praying Psalm 139:23–24 every day?

FROM SUSIE:

It may seem frightening to surrender something that God is asking you to give Him, but remember... you can trust Him!

67.
Cancel your pity parties.

Sometimes life stinks. Like **really**, *really* stinks. You're struggling with school, your coach **picks on** you (and only you) at practice, your best friend says she never wants to talk to you again, and to top it off you **accidentally bleached** an entire load of laundry containing all your **favorite** clothes. At the end of the day all you want is to crawl on the sofa, put on a marathon of your favorite reality show, and eat a huge bowl (okay fine, an entire carton) of ice cream. After all, with the day you've had, you've earned it. **Right?**

Wrong.

My friend, you have the makings of a **pity party**.

Let's face it. Wallowing feels good. Unfortunately, wallowing doesn't benefit you **at all**. It merely harbors **bitterness, self-centeredness, and steals your joy**.

So when circumstances get you down and you're tempted to switch into **woe mode**, throw a different kind of party!

Parties need guests, so **let Jesus crash your pity party**. (That should be on a bumper sticker. Except you probably don't want the word *crash* anywhere on a car.)

Seriously, though. **Pray** and ask Jesus to come give you a godly attitude and the strength to be joyful amidst negative circumstances.

Parties need games, so play a little game of **Truth or Dare** during your pity party. Remind yourself of one of God's **truths**. Like, "He will never leave or forsake me" or "I am fearfully and wonderfully made" and **dare** yourself to do something selfless like fold the laundry, give someone a hug, or write an encouraging thank-you note to a teacher or pastor.

Good parties have food, too. So grab a bowl of ice cream, but stop there. Even better, grab some siblings or some friends and bake a cake to go with your ice cream!

Kristin

• •

FROM GOD:

♥ "Count it all joy, my brothers, when you meet trials of various kinds, for you know that the testing of your faith produces steadfastness" (James 1:2–3 ESV).

♥ "Come to me, all who labor and are heavy laden, and I will give you rest. Take my yoke upon you, and learn from me, for I am gentle and lowly in heart, and you will find rest for your souls. For my yoke is easy, and my burden is light" (Matthew 11:28–30 ESV).

GO AHEAD—ANSWER:

»—→ How often do you slip into "pity party" mode? What usually triggers it?

»—→ What's the difference between godly sorrow and a pity party?

»—→ How can you channel your tendency to feel sorry for yourself into something positive and productive?

FROM KRISTIN:

It's not wrong to feel sad. Even Jesus felt sorrow. It's how we handle our sadness that matters.

68.

Learn a skill that would help you survive the apocalypse (e.g., knitting, crocheting, gardening).

When was the last time you ground wheat to **bake bread** from scratch? Or sewed a dress from a pattern? Or grew a full garden of vegetables? With the exception of the Amish and some **homeschoolers**, most people have limited exposure to *homesteading*.

We're so dependent on technology that we rarely experience the satisfaction of doing things the **old-fashioned** way.

Still, we could always lose our technology, electricity, and power, so it's smart to learn a few life-sustaining skills. **Just in case we need them in a post-apocalyptic setting.**

Even if you never need to call upon these skills to **survive**, there're numerous reasons to invest in basic agricultural or domestic knowledge.

- It's **fun** to keep your hands occupied. You can knit or crochet a scarf while watching your favorite movie or hanging out with friends.
- It's an opportunity to express your creativity. There's no limit to the styles, recipes, and gadgets you can create!
- You'll impress elderly people, who believe your generation to be the laziest yet. Better yet, they can probably teach you everything you need to know.
- Food grown by you tastes better. Clothes made with your own two hands are more comfortable. Candles dipped in wax you got from the bees you keep in your backyard shine brighter. (That last one's a stretch. . .but still!)
- You can gain **spiritual insight** from things like gardening. A seed doesn't spring into a mature, fruit-bearing plant overnight. It takes fertile soil, **water**, plant food, weather, **sun**, and time. Sometimes the plant sprouts quickly, other times the growth is so subtle you can barely detect it. **Spiritual growth** is like a seed. Once planted, it needs biblical community, prayer, **time in the Word**, trials, and persistence to grow. Sometimes you grow **quickly**, other times slow. I never would've thought about those comparisons if I hadn't gardened.

- Finally, if we do lose all power, knitting, gardening, and cooking can **fill the hours** left open by our lack of television and Internet.

Kristin

. . . .

FROM GOD:

- ♥ "So neither the one who plants nor the one who waters is anything, but only God, who makes things grow" (1 Corinthians 3:7 NIV).
- ♥ "Be patient, therefore, brothers, until the coming of the Lord. See how the farmer waits for the precious fruit of the earth, being patient about it, until it receives the early and the late rains" (James 5:7 ESV).

GO AHEAD—ANSWER:

»→ Why do you think God uses farming examples in the Bible? What can we learn from farmers?

»→ Do you have any hobbies that involve making things from scratch?

»→ Think about ways you can use your "homesteading" skills to contribute to the body of Christ. Did you come up with anything?

FROM KRISTIN:

In the unlikely event of a zombie apocalypse, these skills would also come in handy. I'm pretty sure you could take out a zombie with a 32-inch knitting needle.

69.

Learn some practical skills to use in nonapocalyptic emergencies —like self-defense, how to change a tire, or unclogging a drain.

There are a few skills that are **extremely valuable** to know in an emergency. Lord willing, you won't ever need them, but keep them in your back pocket, **just in case!**

- **Learn to change a tire and a few basic things about your car.** AAA or other roadside services can help you out, but just in case your phone runs out of battery or you're stranded in a place with no service, you won't be dependent on someone else. Also, knowing a little bit about your car keeps you from getting ripped off at the mechanic's.
- **Learn some self-defense or take karate.** Again, let's hope you never have to use it outside the martial arts center, but knowing how to defend yourself could save your life. Even if you never have to use it, these skills give you confidence and keep you from living in fear.
- **Know how to unclog a drain.** You might actually get to use this one, especially if you possess long hair. If water stops draining in your shower, for example, it means a lovely collection of your hair might've caused a blockage. You'll have to remove the drain stopper and take a Q-tip, hanger end, straightened bobby pin, or other object to reach in and pull out the blockage. It may take several tries, but you'll get it eventually. Pulling out the wad of soap-encrusted hair is one of life's most disgustingly satisfying feelings. Also, your shower will drain again.
- **Take some first aid and CPR classes.** I've heard several stories from people who've had to perform the Heimlich or CPR on a stranger to help save their life. It's also good to know how to recognize the signs of strokes and heart attacks and how to treat basic wounds. You can potentially bless someone else with that knowledge.

Kristin

FROM GOD:

❤ "Why, you do not even know what will happen tomorrow. What is your life? You are a mist that appears for a little while and then vanishes" (James 4:14 NIV).

❤ "The prudent sees danger and hides himself, but the simple go on and suffer for it" (Proverbs 22:3 ESV).

GO AHEAD—ANSWER:

»→ Do you have some practical skills?

»→ Are there any other practical skills that might be useful to know?

»→ Have you ever been in a situation where you've used any of these skills?

FROM KRISTIN:

From my book of personal experience, it's a good idea to keep a fire extinguisher in the kitchen. Trust me.

70.
Memorize scripture.

Part of the Holy Spirit's job description is to reveal **truth** to us. Think of memorizing scripture as putting ammunition in your backpack. The next time you're involved in **conflict**, the Holy Spirit will bring to your mind the exact scripture you need: "You will keep in perfect peace all who trust in you, all whose thoughts are fixed on you!" (Isaiah 26:3 NLT).

OR "I am leaving you with a gift—peace of mind and heart! And the peace I give isn't fragile like the peace the world gives. So don't be troubled or afraid" (John 14:27 TLB).

But the Holy Spirit can only bring to your mind what you've memorized. So the more you **memorize**, the more comfort, peace, and guidance you have when you need it.

Let's say someone asks you how to become a Christian. If you've memorized scripture that promises **salvation** as a free gift, you can share that with your friend. If you don't have it memorized, it's simply you talking.

Think of the Bible as a lamp that **lights the path** before you. No longer do you have to stumble in the darkness; you have God's Word to guide you. Consider it a road map. The Holy Spirit will use the Bible to show you which way to turn when you come to a fork in the road.

To start memorizing scripture, ask your youth leader or pastor to list some verses you should begin with. Copy them on 3x5 cards and carry them with you. Also, place another set in **strategic places** where you'll see them often (on your bathroom mirror, dashboard, the fridge, etc.) and begin memorizing them.

If you can't get with your pastor or youth leader, start with verses on salvation (you can use these when sharing your faith). Then move on to verses about faith, peace, trials, fear. Many Bibles have a great **index** at the back that will be helpful.

The more you memorize scripture and begin to live it, the better equipped you'll be to make wise choices and share your faith.

Susie

FROM GOD:

- ❤ "Thy word is a lamp unto my feet, and a light unto my path" (Psalm 119:105 KJV).
- ❤ "The whole Bible was given to us by inspiration from God and is useful to teach us what is true and to make us realize what is wrong in our lives; it straightens us out and helps us do what is right. It is God's way of making us well prepared at every point, fully equipped to do good to everyone" (2 Timothy 3:16–17 TLB).

GO AHEAD—ANSWER:

- »→ Say out loud as many Bible verses as you can that you have memorized.
- »→ Describe how God's Word has helped you in the past. How would you like to see the Bible used more effectively in your life?
- »→ Will you commit to memorizing a new Bible verse each week for the next year? If so, you'll have fifty-two verses in your heart by this time next year!

FROM SUSIE:

Here's one of my favorite scriptures: "But these things I plan won't happen right away. Slowly, steadily, surely, the time approaches when the vision will be fulfilled. If it seems slow, do not despair, for these things will surely come to pass. Just be patient! They will not be overdue a single day!" (Habakkuk 2:3 TLB)

71.
Cultivate your creativity.

You probably already know that your brain has two sides. The left side handles the detail stuff, and the right side is the creative side. If you're not very good at math and if you're not analytical by nature, you're probably more right-brained.

If you love science, puzzles, and figuring out how things work, you're more left-brained. One side isn't more important than the other side, but learning how to use the right side of your brain more will enable you to make discoveries and enjoy life in a variety of ways.

The left side of your brain will aid you in finding the path to the discovery, but it's your creative side that actually discovers. So how can you learn to engage the right side of your brain?

Take an art class, pick up an instrument, or go to a creative writing workshop. Doing new and different things will unlock the right side of your brain. For example, if you always use the same route driving home, change it up! Take a different street.

If you tend to sit in a specific place in the cafeteria, church, or theater, sit in a completely different section. Forcing yourself to do even small things like this will engage the right side of your brain and keep your thinking sharp and clear.

And the advantage of this? You'll be that much closer to creating a piece of carpet that really can fly, an alarm clock that wakes you up with a hot serving of oatmeal, or teaching your dog to say, "I really like this fun book by Susie and Kristin!"

Susie

* *

FROM GOD:

- ❤ "For we are his workmanship, created in Christ Jesus for good works, which God prepared beforehand, that we should walk in them" (Ephesians 2:10 ESV).
- ❤ "Whatever you do, work at it with all your heart, as working for the Lord, not for human masters" (Colossians 3:23 NIV).

GO AHEAD—ANSWER:

»——→ Are you more left-brained or right-brained? More detailed and organized or more visionary and creative?

»——→ Describe someone who's really creative. What do you admire about this person?

»——→ Are there some areas that you can creatively develop in your life?

FROM SUSIE:

Creativity breeds creativity. The more time you spend reading creative works and hanging out with creative people, the more you'll begin to think out of the box.

72.
Count the cost.

Before buying something, you typically find out what it **costs**. A **smart buyer** then determines whether what they get in exchange is worth the price.

You're not going to pay $100 for a pencil. If you do, it better come equipped with **jetpacks**! On the opposite end of the spectrum, if you found a laptop for $5, you'd suspect there's something **wrong** with it.

Are you ready for something that'll give you major brain overload?

Salvation is completely free, yet it costs you everything.

Think about what following Christ may cost you.

Your friends?

Your family?

Your earthly possessions?

Your status?

Your dreams?

You may give up **everything** to follow Christ, but now let's consider what we get in return.

Forgiveness of sins and right standing with God.

Becoming a daughter of God.

The Holy Spirit living in you.

Confidence that all things, even the bad, are being worked for your good.

Support from a community of believers locally and worldwide.

Unshakeable joy.

A heavenly inheritance that can't be destroyed or taken away.

Eternity in heaven.

Giving up any of our earthly things to get even *one* of these blessings is like paying dryer lint for a mansion on the beach. Are you going to **pass up paradise** in order to **hang on to something you'll only eventually throw away**?

Our lives, family, friends, status, dreams, accomplishments, talents, and possessions aren't worth keeping at the expense of losing our souls.

Kristin

● ●

FROM GOD:

- ♥ "Whoever loves father or mother more than me is not worthy of me, and whoever loves son or daughter more than me is not worthy of me" (Matthew 10:37 ESV).
- ♥ "For what will it profit a man if he gains the whole world and forfeits his soul? Or what shall a man give in return for his soul?" (Matthew 16:26 ESV).

GO AHEAD—ANSWER:

- »—→ Have you given up anything in order to follow Christ?
- »—→ What've you gained by following Christ?
- »—→ How often do you think about what God's given you?

FROM KRISTIN:

Every now and then it's good to think about heaven and all the glory and splendor that's waiting for us. The most exciting thing to think about, though, is getting to meet Jesus face-to-face.

As Christians it's easy to get stuck in the "that's good enough" mentality. We know and believe Christ saved us, but we don't let this truth transform **every area** of our lives.

If Christ has changed you, no part of your life is safe from His work. **This is a good thing!** This means pursuing excellence in *all* areas of life.

- Pursue excellence in your walk with God.

Don't be satisfied to merely read a couple verses and say a quick prayer. **Thirst after the Lord!** Start by asking God to change your heart so that your desires match His will. Set aside a couple days a week to study the scripture deeper. Keep a prayer journal. Go to church and listen, take notes, and reflect on what was said. **Talk to God.** Try to keep His commandments. **Listen to God.**

- Pursue excellence in your home life.

This means **honoring** your parents, being kind and gracious to your siblings, working hard at school and chores, and looking for ways to serve your neighbors.

- Pursue excellence at work.

Do you know one of the easiest ways to impress someone? Don't cancel last-minute and show up on time. Our culture is getting flaky, and it's important to keep your word. Do your job well, even when no one's watching. Remember, you're not just reporting to your boss. You're reporting to God!

- Pursue excellence with your talents and opportunities.

Don't make your talents an idol (see tip #66), but also recognize that God gave them to you for a purpose. Don't let **hard work or fear of failure** keep you from pursuing something.

Kristin

• •

FROM GOD:

♥ "Do you not know that in a race all the runners run, but only one receives the prize? So run that you may obtain it. Every athlete exercises self-control in all things. They do it to receive a perishable wreath, but we an imperishable. So I do not run aimlessly; I do not box as one beating the air. But I discipline my body and keep it under control, lest after preaching to others I myself should be disqualified" (1 Corinthians 9:24–27 ESV).

♥ "As for me, I shall behold your face in righteousness; when I awake, I shall be satisfied with your likeness" (Psalm 17:15 ESV).

GO AHEAD—ANSWER:

»—→ What does it mean to "pursue excellence"?
»—→ What's a talent God gave you that you can use for His Kingdom?
»—→ In what ways have you done a good job pursuing excellence? In what areas do you need to work harder?

FROM KRISTIN:

There's a big difference between contentment and complacency. You can be happy with where God has you while still chasing excellence.

74.
Develop an attitude of gratitude.

I love to smell the inside of new shoes—especially tennis shoes. There's something about the canvas and leather and stitching all coming together in one **fresh smell** that I really like. And the smell of a new car? **Wow!** If they could put that smell in a bottle, I'd wear it as perfume. And the smell of a **just-bathed** baby. And puppy breath. And new-book smell, the savory scent of roast beef simmering in a Crock-Pot, cupcakes as they're baking, new duct tape, and the smell of clean laundry.

I'm amazed at how a wildflower can grow out of a crack in the cement, how a flamingo can stand **on one leg** for so long (and why it even *wants* to stand on one leg when it *has* two! I want to scream, "Use your other leg! It's okay!"), the calm and wonder found in a double rainbow, how **frontiersmen** did it all—made soap, skinned animals for clothing, grew their own food, wrote with charcoal, and lived happily without TV or an iPod or a cell phone—and how a beautiful butterfly can come out of such an ugly thing as a caterpillar—and how it knows *when* to come out—and why rain has such a distinct smell when water is odorless.

I marvel at the fact that **toddlers** can learn a whole language just by listening to those around them, yet I forget the name of someone I've known for years. I love it that gravity works and the sun isn't ten degrees hotter, and I wonder why bowling balls only have three holes instead of five and why it took so long for someone to think of putting wheels on luggage.

I love color—**all colors**—and can't imagine how there are even *more* colors that we haven't seen that fill heaven! It amazes me how wildflowers can grow in the **hottest place** on earth—Death Valley, California (the World Meteorological Organization has officially recognized Death Valley as the world's hottest spot with 136 degrees Fahrenheit as its recorded high), and that people can actually live and work in a research station in the **coldest place** in the world (Vostok, Antarctica, with a record low of -128 degrees Fahrenheit).

What amazes you?

What makes you smile?

What smells take you back to your childhood?

What **sounds** make you giggle?

As you make time to appreciate the little things in life, you'll automatically develop an **attitude of gratitude**. And a grateful person is a happy person.

Susie

FROM GOD:

- 💜 "In every thing give thanks: for this is the will of God in Christ Jesus concerning you" (1 Thessalonians 5:18 KJV).
- 💜 "I thank my God every time I remember you. In all my prayers for all of you, I always pray with joy" (Philippians 1:3–4 NIV).

GO AHEAD—ANSWER:

»—→ When was the last time you thanked God for something simple? (If you can't remember, pause and do it right now.)

»—→ Describe three of your favorite everyday, ordinary things that you truly appreciate.

»—→ Why is it important to be appreciative?

FROM SUSIE:

Saying "I appreciate you" to someone can turn a bad day into a good one. Do that for someone today!

75.
Approach anger with gentleness.

Say you're sitting on your bed, reading an **adventurous** book. The story just took an exciting turn, but before you can find out what happens next, your older sister bursts into your room, demanding to know where you put her favorite top. She *knows* you took it, she yells.

While you've maybe taken her clothes in the past, you haven't *touched* this shirt and have **no idea** what she's talking about. All you know is your sister is *very* angry and falsely accusing you of something you didn't do.

How do you respond?

When someone approaches us in anger we naturally switch into **defensive** mode and respond in anger.

It's the *natural* response, but it's not necessarily the *right* response. The Bible suggests a **different** reaction.

"A soft answer turns away wrath, but a harsh word stirs up anger" (Proverbs 15:1 ESV).

Instead of yelling back, try keeping your voice calm and telling your sister nicely that you haven't seen it. Maybe you can even help her look for it.

Anger is like a fast-spreading **virus**, and with a few exceptions where **righteous anger** may be appropriate, it's not good to get angry.

Righteous anger is getting upset over things that grieve God. Getting angry about abuse, **murder**, bullying, or other injustice is a *right* reaction to sin. Righteous anger has one **big difference** over other anger: it drives us to God, not to lash out at others. Sometimes righteous anger drives us to pitch in to help change things.

In all things, though, we must check our words and actions because we **know God is in control**. We **love** our neighbor and **listen** to their complaints. We **humbly** acknowledge and receive their complaints against us, even if they don't seem fair. We respond with **gentleness**.

If you *do* lose your cool (and let's face it, we're human), apologize for getting angry—even if you weren't initially at fault. A humble, gentle spirit can often neutralize anger.

Kristin

FROM GOD:

- ❤ "To speak evil of no one, to avoid quarreling, to be gentle, and to show perfect courtesy toward all people" (Titus 3:2 ESV).
- ❤ "My dear brothers and sisters, take note of this: Everyone should be quick to listen, slow to speak and slow to become angry" (James 1:19 NIV).

GO AHEAD—ANSWER:

»—→ Has anyone ever responded to your anger with gentleness? What did that do to your anger?

»—→ Have you tried staying calm when someone's angry with you?

»—→ How does knowing we deserve wrath, but instead get mercy, affect the way you respond to anger?

FROM KRISTIN:

When struggling with anger, I remind myself that I deserve God's anger, but instead He gave me mercy through Jesus. This helps me extend grace—even when I don't think someone deserves it!

76.
Wear comfortable shoes.

If there's one piece of advice I can impart to you about fashion, it's **wear comfortable shoes**.

Those sleek red pumps might look like the perfect finish to your outfit *now*, but *later* they'll make you **rue the day** you were born.

When it comes to foot panache, **comfort** trumps **style**. Nothing's worse than being pestered throughout the day by blisters, numb feet, and lack of circulation. You may also get tired of people asking why you're limping.

Plus, as amazing as they make you look, heels give you **back problems**, increase your risk of twisting an ankle (especially if you're klutzy like me), and make maneuvering in general more difficult. Ever watched someone try and go up and down stairs wearing 4-inch wedges? It's hilarious.

If a big event is coming up requiring you to wear fancy shoes for hours, **test them out** ahead of time. It usually only takes an hour or two for those pesky blisters to form, so wear them around the house for a while and make sure they don't irritate your **precious tootsies**.

If you *must* wear stiff, uncomfortable shoes, bring Band-Aids, moleskin, or something else to put over spots irritating your **beautiful bases**.

If you said to yourself, "I hope I get a few other shoe-related nuggets of wisdom before this section ends," you're in luck! Here're a few other insights I've learned along the way:

- Don't break in a new pair of hiking boots on a fourteen-mile hike.
- Don't wear platforms/wedges/pumps if you know you'll be going up and down stairs. (Unless you want to be laughed at.)
- Don't **ever pay retail** for shoes. You can almost always find the same or a similar shoe at a discount shop or online.

Lastly, the *best* shoes are the ones you've worn so long they're duct taped together. It's like having a sole mate. (See what I did there?)

Kristin

FROM GOD:

- ❤ "Turn my eyes from looking at worthless things; and give me life in your ways" (Psalm 119:37 ESV).
- ❤ "As it is written, 'How beautiful are the feet of those who preach the good news!' " (Romans 10:15 ESV).

GO AHEAD—ANSWER:

- »—→ Do you favor comfort or style in your shoe choices?
- »—→ Do you think God cares about the smallest details, like what shoes you wear? Why or why not?
- »—→ How many pairs of shoes do you own? How many do you think you need?

FROM KRISTIN:

This chapter exhausted my list of synonyms for feet.

77.
Remind yourself there's a world outside of high school.

Adults often refer to kids as **future leaders**. I dislike this thinking. I don't want you to wait until after high school to start leading. **I want you to begin now.**

When you're sitting alone at lunch, trying to fit in, and **stressing out** over assignments and tests, remind yourself that someday school will end and focus on using these years for God's Kingdom.

1. View school as a unique opportunity to witness.

You're not just sitting in class, practicing with the orchestra, or representing Bolivia at Model UN. You're among people who **don't know Jesus**. No one has the same access to these kids as you, and you may rarely see them again after graduation. It's a **powerful opportunity** to share the gospel with both your words and the way you live your life.

2. Don't act the way culture expects teens to act.

Instead of partying, gossiping, dating around, and slacking off, start intentionally growing in the Lord now—don't wait until you're older. **Join a church**, read the Bible, and hang around with godly people. **Act in a way** that shows you're a new creation in Christ, not just a typical teenager.

3. School is temporary. Stay focused on things that are eternal.

After high school it won't matter if you're captain of the cheerleading squad or prom queen. Your popularity, or lack thereof, won't carry over into post-school life.

What *will* carry over is the character built during these years. Did you work hard in your classes? Did you learn how to manage your time? Did you stand firm in your faith? Did you share Jesus with your friends? Did you put God first?

Those traits, my friends, are things that make the high school years worth it.

Kristin

• •

FROM GOD:

♥ "Let no one despise you for your youth, but set the believers an example in speech, in conduct, in love, in faith, in purity" (1 Timothy 4:12 ESV).

♥ "Remember also your Creator in the days of your youth" (Ecclesiastes 12:1 ᴇꜱᴠ).

GO AHEAD—ANSWER:

»—→ Are you currently representing Christ well at your school?
»—→ Do you act one way at church and another around your peers? What's stopping you from acting the right way?
»—→ Why do you think it's important to view yourself as a leader now?

FROM KRISTIN:

I've heard some incredible testimonies from older people whom God saved through being loved and witnessed to by youth. Don't take these years for granted—you can greatly impact society before you're even old enough to vote!

78.
Learn to juggle.

Have you ever been **standing around** at a get-together thinking, *Sheesh, I wish I knew a quick, fun way to entertain people.* (By the way, you get ten points for using *sheesh* in a sentence.)

Some things in life are worth learning solely because they're **fun and awesome**. Juggling falls into that category.

You can easily YouTube a juggling tutorial, find a how-to-juggle book, or ask someone who already knows how to teach you.

It takes a little while to learn, but the **benefits** far outweigh the effort you'll put into it. You can quickly entertain your friends at parties, amuse the kids you're babysitting, or put on some clown makeup and make some extra cash as a birthday party entertainer!

As a bonus, juggling also gives you a mild workout.

Want some other ideas about **fun things** to spend time learning?

- Learn to play the **ukulele**. It's portable and easy to learn!
- Memorize some **fun trivia** to share.
- Learn some **jokes** to tell the group.
- Learn to ride a **unicycle**.
- Learn some simple **card tricks**.

Kristin

. . . .

FROM GOD:

- ❤ "Also that everyone should eat and drink and take pleasure in all his toil—this is God's gift to man" (Ecclesiastes 3:13 ESV).
- ❤ "Each one's work will become manifest, for the Day will disclose it, because it will be revealed by fire, and the fire will test what sort of work each one has done" (1 Corinthians 3:13 ESV).

GO AHEAD—ANSWER:

»——→ What are some fun things you enjoy doing with your friends?

»——→ Do you have any special talents or "tricks" up your sleeve?

»——→ It's not about bringing attention to yourself; it's about bringing joy to others! What other ways do you like bringing joy to people?

FROM KRISTIN:

Here's a hint to get you started: begin by juggling scarves! They don't fall as fast, so it gives you more time to coordinate the motions.

FROM SUSIE:

I can juggle two tennis balls. In one hand.

79.
Do your best in school, but don't obsess over grades.

There's a lot of pressure on kids these days to be **academic rock stars**. Our culture places a lot of worth and value in an education and a high GPA.

It *is* important to work hard in school. You've been given the opportunity to learn. In the past, education was a luxury not everyone could afford. Don't take this for granted, but don't feel like a failure if you're not a straight-A student.

There are many ways we can spend our time each day. Between **school**, family, **church**, extracurricular activities, and **hobbies**, we can start getting spread pretty thin. I'd suggest sitting down and talking with your parents about what's expected of you regarding school, after-school activities, and other commitments. Then whatever you agree on, work hard in these areas and don't stress too much if you get a B or C here and there.

It's okay not to be in all AP classes. (In fact, you could go take classes at a community college over the summer and be guaranteed college credit.)

If you're in high school and know you want to pursue a particular degree or career path, it may be a good idea to see what their GPA and other academic requirements are for entrance into those programs and focus on those areas rather than trying to be the best at everything.

The bottom line is this: **don't slack, but don't stress either**. Do your best with the time and talents God's given you. We're not all going to be math whizzes or amazing writers. There are many other important aspects of life outside the walls of a classroom. Volunteering at your church or a place like Big Brothers Big Sisters, spending quality time with your family, or getting a job all teach you powerful lessons. Lessons that can't be recognized by letter grades.

Kristin

• •

FROM GOD:

♥ "For the one who sows to his own flesh will from the flesh reap corruption, but the one who sows to the Spirit will from the Spirit reap eternal life" (Galatians 6:8 ESV).

❤ "A new commandment I give to you, that you love one another: just as I have loved you, you also are to love one another" (John 13:34 ESV).

GO AHEAD—ANSWER:

»⟶ How are you in school? Are you a workaholic, slacker, or in the middle?

»⟶ Are grades important? Why or why not?

»⟶ What are some life lessons you can learn from school? (Example: time management.)

FROM KRISTIN:

I'm thankful I got to learn math. I'm also thankful I've rarely had to use it in everyday life.

FROM SUSIE:

I'm convinced there are three types of people in the world: those who are good at math. . . and those who aren't.

80.
Smell good.

I love perfume, and I have several favorite scents. The problem with perfume is—as great as it smells—it can be expensive. So sometimes I get my scents at Bath & Body Works. They're a lot less expensive than regular **perfume**, and they have some great scents.

It's not only fun to smell good, but people love hanging around someone who smells good. **Don't**, however, use perfume or body sprays instead of taking a shower! Trying to cover up a bad smell with a good smell only makes the smell **worse**.

Of course, if you're allergic to perfume, just ignore this tip! A few years ago I noticed a great **fragrance** that a friend of mine was wearing. I asked what it was and bought a bottle. I started wearing it and immediately loved it. But after a couple of days I started **itching**. In fact, throughout the day, I was **scratching** below my ears and on my neck—the exact places I had sprayed my new scent. Unfortunately, I had developed a rash from the perfume and was obviously allergic to it.

I loved the scent so much, I continued wearing it until the rash became unbearable and I had to stop. I waited **several months** and tried it again but had the same results. You'd think I'd learn, wouldn't you? I waited **two years** and tried again (I *really* loved this fragrance!), but developed the rash almost as soon as I sprayed it on.

I finally gave up and now wear a pot roast around my neck. (See tip #45.) I smell great!

Susie

• •

FROM GOD:

- ♥ "For we are to God the pleasing aroma of Christ among those who are being saved and those who are perishing" (2 Corinthians 2:15 NIV).
- ♥ "I am the way and the truth and the life. No one comes to the Father except through me" (John 14:6 NIV).

GO AHEAD—ANSWER:

»⟶ What are three of your favorite smells?

»⟶ What actions "smell like God"?

»⟶ How can you live your life to be a pleasing aroma to Christ?

FROM SUSIE:

As much as I love smells (see tip #74), I desire even more to develop a lifestyle that's a pleasing aroma to my heavenly Father. That's an eternal smell-good!

81.
Go to the ant, you sluggard. (Don't be lazy.)

"Go to the ant, you sluggard; consider its ways and be wise!" (Proverbs 6:6 NIV).

Have you ever **accidentally** stepped on an ant pile? If you're from an area where fire ants live, you **probably** sprint as fast as possible in the opposite direction. (For those of you who've never seen a fire ant, they're vile little creatures named for their fire-like bites.)

If you stick around to watch the ants, though, you'll discover they work quickly, efficiently, and tirelessly to repair the damage done to their home.

It's **easy** to get lazy in today's culture. We have **Facebook**, Twitter, **Pinterest**, 650 channels on television, YouTube, hundreds of thousands of movies to watch, malls to get lost in, blogs, **tabloids**, magazines, and many, **many** other entertainment outlets. We could go through life **merely being entertained**, never thinking an original thought, creating a piece of art, or contributing to something bigger than ourselves. That's not what the ants teach us, though.

Let's see what **positive traits** we can learn from these little critters:

- They **work together** to build their colonies.
- They **diligently** collect and store food for the winter.
- They **don't procrastinate**. The instant a human foot tramples their home they **spring to action**.
- They can **lift** several times their own body weight.

Now think about your own life. Do you work together with others to accomplish things? Do you get things finished immediately or do you wait until the **last minute** and do a halfhearted job? Do you spend more time **daydreaming** than **doing**?

When you're at work, show up on time, **do your absolute best**, and help out your coworkers. When something needs to get done, **do it immediately and do it well**. If you have a dream or a goal, **stop thinking about it and start planning how you can reach it**.

The same goes for your **spiritual life**. If you're lazy, don't study the Bible, never pray, or don't hang around godly people, you **suffer spiritually**. Those who work diligently and **pursue God** see beautiful fruit! And not the kind ants can carry off and store for the winter.

Kristin

FROM GOD:

- ♥ "The soul of the sluggard craves and gets nothing, while the soul of the diligent is richly supplied" (Proverbs 13:4 ESV).
- ♥ "For even when we were with you, we would give you this command: If anyone is not willing to work, let him not eat" (2 Thessalonians 3:10 ESV).

GO AHEAD—ANSWER:

»—→ In what areas of your life have you let yourself slack off? Work? School? Spiritually?

»—→ Does your work ethic reflect Christ? Do you do just enough to please people, or do you do your absolute best to please God?

»—→ Is there anything you're currently putting off because it's too hard? How can you get started?

FROM KRISTIN:

If you have a little spare time on your hands after working hard in all you do, go find some ants to watch for inspiration. Just steer clear of those fire ants.

82.
Learn to know God's will for your life.

When I was in the fourth grade, we studied Lewis and Clark—great American explorers. **That did it.** I decided I wanted to be an explorer. By the time I was in fifth grade, I wanted to be a nurse. And then a doctor. But although I was okay with blood, I wasn't okay with math, chemistry, or anything you really need to know about the medical field.

Oftentimes when we think about God's will for our lives, we tend to think about what **career** He wants us to pursue. Although our career is certainly part of God's will for our lives, it's not the total picture. His will for your life **right now** is that you become as close to Him as you can get. You can do that through reading your Bible, being a part of a loving church family who will **nurture** you in your relationship with Christ, and by developing a strong prayer life.

God's will for your life **right now** is also that you share Him with others. We're mentioning this a few times in this book because it's really important that you let those around you know how much God loves them. You don't have to preach; just live a happy life in Christ. And when they ask you why you're so happy, let them know it's because of God.

There are times, however, when we need to discern God's will about a specific situation. Remember the following:

- **God's will is found in God's Word.** He will speak to you through the Bible.
- **God's will isn't a feeling.** Feelings aren't good or bad—just don't depend on them to know God's will for your life.
- **God's will is revealed to you through prayer.** Ask Him what He wants you to do in this situation.

God is so faithful. He won't leave you hanging! He will guide you.

Susie

• •

FROM GOD:

- ❤ "I take joy in doing your will, my God, for your instructions are written on my heart" (Psalm 40:8 NLT).
- ❤ "The effective, fervent prayer of a righteous man avails much" (James 5:16 NKJV).

GO AHEAD—ANSWER:

»→ Is there a specific area in your life in which you struggle in discerning God's will?

»→ Describe a time you sought His guidance, and He showed you what to do.

»→ Can we always count on God to lead us if we seek His direction?

FROM SUSIE:

Oftentimes God's will coincides with the desires of our heart. And when we live in the center of His will, He places those desires within us. In other words. . .His desires become our desires.

83.
Sing in the shower.

Do you enjoy singing? Of *course* you do! Everyone does. If people didn't love singing so much, **American Idol** wouldn't be in its hundredth season. (That may be a slight exaggeration—but I've stopped keeping count.)

Singing is a wonderful way to lift your spirits, worship God, and express joy.

Plus, I bet you didn't realize you have your *own* personal stage, complete with a microphone and great acoustics.

It's called the shower!

That's right. The shower transforms even the worst singer into a Broadway star.

It's time to make a joyful noise and get clean! Think of your favorite worship songs. Here are some personal favorites to get you started:

"Give Us Clean Hands" (adds a dash of irony)

"How Great Thou Art"

"Come, Now Is the Time to Worship"

Unless you shower at 5 a.m. when everyone's sleeping, it isn't the time to be shy. Belt those lyrics out! Shout to the Lord!

If singing aloud for fun isn't enough of a reason, deeply inhaling steam is good for your throat and sinus cavities!

Now, go make a joyful noise!

Kristin

. . . .

FROM GOD:

♥ "Make a joyful noise to the Lord, all the earth! Serve the Lord with gladness! Come into his presence with singing!" (Psalm 100:1–2 ESV).

♥ "Praise the Lord! For it is good to sing praises to our God; for it is pleasant, and a song of praise is fitting" (Psalm 147:1 ESV).

GO AHEAD—ANSWER:

»—→ Are you shy singing in front of people, or will you pump the pipes in front of anyone?

»—→ What are your favorite praise and worship songs to sing?

»—→ Why do you think songs are used to praise God?

FROM KRISTIN:

I enjoy singing at the top of my lungs in the shower, in my car, in the grocery store, anywhere! I always bring complimentary earplugs to give to those around me.

84.
Learn to be okay alone.

I have ridden a camel at the Great Wall of China, snorkeled Australia's Great Barrier Reef, Jet-Skied in the Indian Ocean, been on an African safari, eaten guinea pig, spent time in the jungle of Irian Jaya, visited a leper colony in India, hiked in the Swiss Alps, kayaked in Antarctica, and have visited every continent in the world.

God has allowed me to have some **amazing** adventures. Most of these adventures have been connected with ministry. I've led more than six thousand students on mission trips during the last several years. Following God is incredibly exciting!

I've often **wondered** if I would've been able to do all He has allowed me to do if I weren't single. The apostle Paul said that when we're single it's easier to **wholeheartedly** devote ourselves to the Lord's work because we don't have responsibilities to a spouse or family. I've certainly realized this to be true in my own life.

I hope someday God will bring **marriage** into my life, but until He does, I'm having the time of my life simply serving Him and experiencing the adventures He's bringing my way.

Learn to be okay with being alone. Don't be someone who's so **dependent** on other people that you don't feel whole unless you're with someone else. **You can be whole with Christ.**

Too often people enter marriage thinking, *My spouse will make me whole.* After all, don't two halves make a whole? In math, they do; in marriage, they don't. Marriage is about **one whole person** marrying another whole person and creating one whole union.

Right now—during your teen years—is the time to learn how to be whole with Christ. Then when He brings the right man into your life, you'll already **be whole** and ready for marriage.

Learn to feel confident with just having Christ by your side. Feel good about walking into the cafeteria **alone**, going to a basketball game alone, getting a pizza alone. You're never *really* alone because **Christ** is with you!

Susie

FROM GOD:

❤ "Wives, submit to your own husbands, as to the Lord. For the husband is the head of the wife even as Christ is the head of the church, his body, and is himself its Savior. Now as the church submits to Christ, so also wives should submit in everything to their husbands. Husbands, love your wives, as Christ loved the church and gave himself up for her, that he might sanctify her, having cleansed her by the washing of water with the word" (Ephesians 5:22–26 ESV).

❤ "Do not be unequally yoked with unbelievers. For what partnership has righteousness with lawlessness? Or what fellowship has light with darkness?" (2 Corinthians 6:14 ESV).

GO AHEAD—ANSWER:

»→ How many children would you like to have someday?

»→ Do you see yourself being married right out of college, or do you see yourself in a career first?

»→ Discuss the advantages of serving God through marriage. Discuss the advantages of serving Him through singleness.

FROM SUSIE:

I believe the greatest thing God invented is marriage. Without it, we wouldn't be here! It's an amazing reflection of His union with the Church. It's a high calling to be a wife and mother—to nurture your husband and disciple your children. But until God brings that into your life, learn to be happy, content, and WHOLE in your relationship with Christ.

85.
Be fearless.

There's one emotion that seems to rule them all: **fear**.

Did you know in the Bible we're only supposed to fear **one thing**?

"The fear of the LORD is a fountain of life, that one may turn away from the snares of death" (Proverbs 14:27 ESV).

Fearing the Lord isn't the type of fear where you end up cowering in the corner. It's more of the awe and reverence that's associated with recognizing Him as the creator and sustainer of the universe. If we have *this* fear, then all other fears (which *can* send us cowering into a corner) should be put away.

Are you **afraid** of sharing the gospel?

Are you afraid of visiting a youth group because you don't know anyone?

Are you afraid of standing up for someone who's being bullied?

Are you afraid of trying out for the school play?

Are you afraid of pursuing a career because it's competitive and you might fail?

Fear is natural. Sometimes it's even **healthy**. People who don't feel fear are often reckless and end up in the hospital after trying to do a flip off the roof on their bike.

But we're not supposed to fear the future, pursuing things we're called to do, or having our needs met. God promises to take care of us.

Sometimes you have to *act* fearless before you *feel* fearless.

We've talked a lot about putting our hope and security in Christ. If that's where your treasure is, then you have nothing to lose by getting out there and sharing the gospel, trying new things, and standing up for what's right. **No earthly failure** can take away your salvation, God's love for you, or your worth. The worst it can do is make you feel humiliated for a little bit. And that seems terrible at the time, but it's not so bad.

When you start to feel fear, **pray** to God and ask Him to remove it. Pray for courage to do the right thing in spite of fear. The Holy Spirit is faithful. He'll be right there with you, giving you boldness like you've never experienced before.

Kristin

FROM GOD:

- ♥ "When I am afraid, I put my trust in you" (Psalm 56:3 ESV).
- ♥ "Be strong and courageous. Do not fear or be in dread of them, for it is the LORD your God who goes with you. He will not leave you or forsake you" (Deuteronomy 31:6 ESV).

GO AHEAD—ANSWER:

»—→ What types of things do you fear?

»—→ How should we approach and handle fear as believers?

»—→ Name three things you can do next time you're tempted to act or react out of fear.

FROM KRISTIN:

My biggest fear is that I'll reach the end of my life, look back, and see that I let my fears run my life.

86.

Don't eat something that's been sitting in the pantry for years without first examining the contents.

When I was a teenager, I'd often go into our walk-in pantry to find a snack. When extremely hungry, I wouldn't even bother taking my food out into the kitchen. I'd stand right there in the pantry and eat it. (A little odd, I know.)

Once during a particularly hungry and lazy moment, I walked into the pantry, not even troubling to turn the light on, and grabbed a bag of walnuts that'd been sitting on the pantry shelf for as long as I could remember.

I began popping the walnuts into my mouth, thinking about what else I might want to eat while in there. I reached in to grab another nut when I felt something move in the bag.

Uh-oh, I thought to myself. *I don't remember walnuts being squirmy.*

I flicked on the light, looked into the bag, and what did my eyes behold? None other than swarms of tiny little moths and larvae.

I screamed and dropped the bag. As the bag hit the ground, moths exploded out of it and scattered to all corners of the pantry. The ancestors of these moths are still living in my parents' pantry to this day, probably now into the eight-hundredth generation. (I'm not sure how moth genealogy works, but that sounds about right.) I still cringe every time I see a moth.

There are numerous little lessons you can glean from this strange tale:

- Be observant. Actually look at what you're eating.
- Don't be lazy. Take the extra two seconds and turn the lights on.
- Throw away old food. Better yet, try and consume it by its expiration date so you don't waste.
- Get rid of pantry moths immediately; otherwise their ancestors will haunt you for the rest of your life.
- Be diligent in every area of life, even if it's something small like grabbing a snack.

And the most important lesson? Eating moths doesn't kill you. It might even make you stronger.

Kristin

FROM GOD:

- ❤ "But when anything is exposed by the light, it becomes visible, for anything that becomes visible is light. Therefore it says, 'Awake, O sleeper, and arise from the dead, and Christ will shine on you'" (Ephesians 5:13–14 ESV).
- ❤ "The desire of the sluggard kills him, for his hands refuse to labor" (Proverbs 21:25 ESV).

GO AHEAD—ANSWER:

»⟶ What's the most disgusting thing you've eaten?

»⟶ What are some smaller areas of life that you may have gotten lazy in? Brushing your teeth? Eating right? What might some of the consequences be?

»⟶ Pray and ask God to shine light in areas of your life that might need a little tweaking.

FROM KRISTIN:

If you know how to get rid of pantry moths, let me know. Shouting, "Away! Away, ye blasphemous moths!" in a Shakespearean dialect doesn't work. I've tried.

87.
Be careful what you feed your brain.

You might've heard the popular catch phrase, "You are what you eat."

Well, the same can be said of your brain. You are what you watch. And listen to. And look at.

Too much junk food makes your body unhealthy. Too much junk media makes your brain unhealthy.

Everything that goes into our mind comes out somehow. It either surfaces as a lie we end up believing, a behavior we adopt, or a lens through which we view the world. Sometimes we don't even realize it's happening.

There's a kids' channel on television, and nearly every show on this network shows the children treating the adults disrespectfully and getting away with it. What do you think kids start believing when they see parents and other authority figures constantly portrayed as stupid? Sure, it may play into the comedy aspect of the show, but the overall message is, "Adults are idiots, and we don't have to listen to them or honor them."

I've spoken with several parents who've stopped letting their kids watch this channel because they began treating adults the same as the characters on the show. Nobody directly told them to treat their parents this way. They merely learned from observation.

This subliminal messaging doesn't stop with age. If you watch too many romantic comedies, you'll expect unrealistic things from your relationships. Many people believe they're entitled to the perfect, flawless, excitement-filled romances they've seen in the movies. In reality, marriage contains some hard work and sacrifice not shown in most Hollywood films.

"Finally, brothers, whatever is true, whatever is honorable, whatever is just, whatever is pure, whatever is lovely, whatever is commendable, if there is any excellence, if there is anything worthy of praise, think about these things" (Philippians 4:8 ESV).

Weigh all your media choices against the above verse. Does the book you're reading encourage justice and morality, or is it merely a love story that puts your thoughts where they shouldn't go? Is the message of the film one of redemption or one that rewards sinful behavior? Are the lyrics of that song pure or filthy?

Poor media choices affect our hearts poorly. They'll increase temptation, decrease satisfaction, play into fantasies, and make us justify sin.

Some things you **can't help** hearing or seeing, like foul language at a sports game or tasteless billboards. But to think you won't be affected by constantly feeding your brain things that contain lies, don't show the consequences of sin, and devalue purity? My friends, that is **simply not wise**.

Kristin

● ●

FROM GOD:

❤ "I will ponder the way that is blameless. Oh when will you come to me? I will walk with integrity of heart within my house; I will not set before my eyes anything that is worthless. I hate the work of those who fall away; it shall not cling to me. A perverse heart shall be far from me; I will know nothing of evil" (Psalm 101:2–4 ESV).

❤ "We are from God. Whoever knows God listens to us; whoever is not from God does not listen to us. By this we know the Spirit of truth and the spirit of error" (1 John 4:6 ESV).

GO AHEAD—ANSWER:

»—→ What kinds of movies do you watch? What kind of music do you listen to? What do you read?

»—→ Think about how you answered the above questions. Which of your media choices do you think honor God? Which ones do you think you should cut out?

»—→ It's hard to find good, clean media in our culture. Take a second to pray and ask God to put Christians in Hollywood to influence the entertainment industry.

FROM KRISTIN:

If you're not sure if something is okay to watch, listen to, or read, try asking a parent or youth leader their thoughts. There're also many online resources for finding out information on something ahead of time. Try Preview Online and Plugged In.

88.
Keep in mind that Jesus is coming again soon!

If you're babysitting and you know the parents are on their way home, **what do you do?** A good babysitter makes sure the house is in order, messes are picked up, and the kids are clean, playing nicely, or sleeping.

Jesus tells us He's coming again soon. He doesn't give us an **exact time, He only tells us to be ready**.

"Therefore you also must be ready, for the Son of Man is coming at an hour you do not expect" (Matthew 24:44 ESV).

What can we do to prepare for Jesus' return?

Fight sin.

Worship God.

Study the Word.

Love sacrificially.

Pray.

Share the gospel.

Be joyful.

Be thankful.

Don't get caught up in the things of the world.

Don't put these things off until later! We aren't guaranteed tomorrow. Jesus is coming again for us **soon!**

Soon.

Soon.

Kristin

• •

FROM GOD:

💜 "Behold, I am coming soon, bringing my recompense with me, to repay each one for what he has done. I am the Alpha and the Omega, the first and the last, the beginning and the end" (Revelation 22:12–13 ESV).

💜 "But concerning that day and hour no one knows, not even the angels of heaven, nor the Son, but the Father only" (Matthew 24:36 ESV).

GO AHEAD—ANSWER:

>→ Why don't you think God wants us to know when Jesus will return?

>→ Are you living like you're expecting Jesus to come at any time?

>→ If you aren't living in a way pleasing to the Lord, what's stopping you from changing?

FROM KRISTIN:

Thinking about Jesus' return gives me goose bumps! I can't wait for the day when our faith becomes sight.

89.
Take a Sabbath.

Have you noticed life can get a little busy? Between school, **chores**, work, **family time**, and church activities, it leaves little time for us to sit, be still, and enjoy God.

The entire first chapter of Genesis tells us about how God created the world. **Now look at the beginning of chapter two.** What does God do after spending six days creating the world? **He rests.** He took a day to enjoy and bask in what He'd done the previous six days.

In the Old Testament the Sabbath fell on sunset Friday to sunset Saturday. The Israelites were **required** to observe it, and God arranged it so they had a full day to devote to Him. Now that Jesus has come, we find our rest in Him and we're not required to observe a specific day or time off anymore. But let's **look at the reason behind the law**. Why did God command a Sabbath?

The Sabbath was rest with a purpose. God wired us and knew we'd need a break from our hard work, so He modeled for us a day of rest. Six days we work, one day we relax, recover, and enjoy God and His creation.

Your Sabbath isn't a time to veg out in front of the television or get consumed in video games. It's also not a time for you to take off from obeying your parents, studying the Word, or doing good. It's a chance to **take a break** from the things of the world and refocus our thoughts and actions on God. Focusing on God prepares us for the week and reminds us of what's important.

Pick activities opposite of what you do all week. If you spend most of your time sitting in a classroom, go do something outdoors. If you're outside playing sports constantly all week, go read or journal at the library. Do things that refresh you spiritually, mentally, and physically.

Kristin

. . . .

FROM GOD:

- ♥ "And he said to them, 'The Sabbath was made for man, not man for the Sabbath' " (Mark 2:27 ESV).
- ♥ "One person esteems one day as better than another, while another esteems all days alike. Each one should be fully convinced in his own mind" (Romans 14:5 ESV).

GO AHEAD—ANSWER:

»——→ Do you have a time of rest each week? Why or why not?
»——→ Explain in your own words the reason God gave us the Sabbath.
»——→ What does your Sabbath look like?

FROM KRISTIN:

My favorite thing to do on my day off is to cook a meal from scratch and, if the weather is warm, spend time outside.

FROM SUSIE:

My fave thing to do on Sunday afternoons is to nap.

90.
Make reasonable goals then complete them.

It happens every year. When the clock strikes midnight on January 1, people make huge, outrageous resolutions they plan on completing during the course of the year. People love the idea of a fresh start and the concept of dreaming big.

"No more sugar, ever!"

"Run ten miles every day!"

"Read the Bible for an hour every day. No excuses!"

I know, I know. We've already told you to dream big. Keep dreaming big, but take realistic steps to achieving those dreams! These goals aren't bad, but usually a few weeks into the New Year our goals get abandoned and we revert to our old habits. You eat a cookie, forget to read the Bible one day, or miss your run, and rather than picking up and pressing on, you quit altogether. Your slate, after all, is no longer clean.

Lofty goals are fun in theory, but it often takes a series of persistent, smaller, less-exciting actions to reach those big goals. Most goals don't get achieved overnight. Or even in a year's time.

If you haven't been exercising, it's unreasonable to expect that you can go from couch potato to marathoner overnight.

Instead, take baby steps. Baby steps still move you in the right direction. Try making smaller goals you can achieve more quickly.

"Eat only one sugary snack a day."

"Run for twenty minutes four days a week."

"Study the Bible for twenty minutes, five days a week."

Once you achieve your smaller goals, you can upgrade from baby steps to larger strides.

"Eat fruit instead of sugar."

"Run thirty minutes three times a week and do a longer distance on the weekend."

"Study the Bible for half an hour each day."

Once your goals are set, put a plan of attack in place to help you achieve them.

"Keep sugary foods out of the house."

"Lay out my workout clothes before going to bed, and set an alarm."

"Set a reminder on my phone so I don't forget to read my Bible!"

Life isn't a sprint. It's a marathon. If you miss a day or a week or even a month, don't get discouraged! Jump right back in where you left off and **keep going**.

Kristin

• •

FROM GOD:

♥ "Therefore, since we are surrounded by so great a cloud of witnesses, let us also lay aside every weight, and sin which clings so closely, and let us run with endurance the race that is set before us, looking to Jesus, the founder and perfecter of our faith, who for the joy that was set before him endured the cross, despising the shame, and is seated at the right hand of the throne of God" (Hebrews 12:1–2 ESV).

♥ "Seek the LORD and his strength; seek his presence continually!" (1 Chronicles 16:11 ESV).

GO AHEAD—ANSWER:

»⟶ Have you ever achieved a big goal? How long did it take? What kind of setbacks did you experience?

»⟶ What are some of your current goals? Do you have a plan to help you achieve them?

»⟶ Do you ever get discouraged in your spiritual "race"? What're some "steps" you can take to help you persevere in your walk with Christ?

FROM KRISTIN:

The most important goal you can have is to grow in your love and knowledge of God. This is a goal we won't officially complete until we die or Jesus comes back, but the reward will be great!

91.
Don't procrastinate.

Ah, we'll come back to this one later.

Susie

• •

92.
Shop at thrift stores.

There's a trove of buried treasure sitting in your community, and the only map you need to find it is your GPS.

It's called the **thrift store**.

Shopping at a thrift store is the modern-day equivalent of **panning for gold**. You sift through a lot of ordinary stuff, but sometimes you find a priceless item that you'll hang on to for the rest of your life.

You'll appreciate this treasure even more because you had to **search** for it, **and it'll likely only cost you $2**.

Plus, each thrift shop item comes with a **story** that *you* get to **create**.

Once while shopping at a thrift shop I found a **visor** for fifty cents. This was **no ordinary visor**, though. The hat's bill is about three times longer than the average visor. It's quite **comical** to see it worn. I break it out at gatherings, use it in skits, and wear it just to cheer people up.

I **imagine** it belonged to a clown before I owned it, and this clown wore it while performing at birthday parties, in hospitals, and sometimes as a street performer in the city. Then one day while walking home from work, a couple of mean crooks jumped out and demanded he hand over his money. He'd just been paid for *two* birthday parties and needed that money for rent. He **refused** to hand it over and ran as fast as he could, which is hard to do in clown shoes. He tripped and lost his hat. He got away, but the hat got left sitting cold and all alone on the sidewalk. Someone passing by saw the hat, picked it up, and threw it in their bag of old clothes going to Goodwill, where I found it.

Now the hat has a safe home in my closet, where it's once again appreciated and used to make people happy.

It's a very loved hat, but I imagine the clown is still searching for it. If I ever see him, I'll give it back. Or maybe we can file for joint hat custody.

Kristin

. . . .

FROM GOD:

💛 "The kingdom of heaven is like treasure hidden in a field. When a man found it, he hid it again, and then in his joy went and sold all he had and bought that field" (Matthew 13:44 NIV).

❤ "If you seek it like silver and search for it as for hidden treasures, then you will understand the fear of the LORD and find the knowledge of God" (Proverbs 2:4–5 ESV).

GO AHEAD—ANSWER:

»——→ Have you shopped at thrift stores before? What treasures have you found?

»——→ We can search for material treasure, but the Bible says to search for eternal things like wisdom and knowledge. How can you search for those things?

»——→ Jesus says the kingdom of heaven is like a treasure hidden in a field. What do you think He means? What is this Treasure worth to you?

FROM KRISTIN:

Thrift shops are a reminder that old junk can become a new treasure—just like us when we put our trust in Christ!

93.
Get involved at church.

Have you ever said or heard someone say, **"I left that church because I wasn't getting anything out of it."**

The very first question I ask people who complain to me about a church is, **"How were you involved?"**

There're legitimate reasons to leave a church, such as when they stop preaching and practicing the truth of scripture. Very often, though, people who grow dissatisfied with a church **aren't serving**. They go to church merely to get something out of it, never giving anything back.

Church isn't **something you can just watch from the stands**. You can know a lot about football, but are you *actually* helping your team win by sitting on a bleacher? **Nope!** It's the people who are down on the field, throwing the ball, **coaching**, getting water, and strategizing the plays who help the team win. You can be excited for your team, **but you can't say you helped**.

By serving your church, you're **actively helping** your local body of Christ advance God's Kingdom. **You're** *in the game.*

Serving **helps** shape you **more** like Christ as you put the best interest of the church ahead of your own comforts and needs.

As you serve you'll find the sermons getting richer, the people getting friendlier, and your soul more fulfilled. Church is no longer about **your need to feel good** at the end of a sermon, but about **God being glorified.**

Kristin

• •

FROM GOD:

♥ "In all things I have shown you that by working hard in this way we must help the weak and remember the words of the Lord Jesus, how he himself said, 'It is more blessed to give than to receive' " (Acts 20:35 ESV).

♥ "Even as the Son of Man came not to be served but to serve, and to give his life as a ransom for many" (Matthew 20:28 ESV).

GO AHEAD—ANSWER:

»⟶ Are you currently serving in your church? If so, in what area?
If not, why?

»⟶ How're you blessed when you serve?

»⟶ Take a moment and think of some ways you can serve your church
and your local body of Christ right now.

FROM KRISTIN:

Serving's a great way to be around people who
you wouldn't meet if it weren't for your mutual
love of folding bulletins or playing with toddlers.

94.
Be a good listener.

Scoot a little closer.

I'm going to let you in on a huge secret.

It's a **surefire plan** for having more friends!

Here's the secret: learn to listen. And listen really really well. People *love* having friends who genuinely know how to listen. Being a good listener doesn't mean simply not saying anything while the other person goes on and on.

Being a good listener involves talking, too, but good listening also means **absorbing** what the other person is saying. It's trying your best to understand what they're communicating. And it's clarifying what they're saying.

For example, if Natasha is telling you how **angry** she is because Maci told Jacqueline that she's crushing on Caleb, it's okay for you to clarify and make sure you understand what she's really saying. She's *telling* you that she's angry, but you **suspect** there's really something deeper going on underneath all that anger. So you can clarify by saying, "If I'm hearing you correctly, you're really hurting because Maci broke your confidence. Is that right?"

Now you've gotten to the **root** of the problem: hurt. Yes, the hurt has led to anger, but now you have a place to start. Could it be that Maci was simply excited about the fact that Natasha liked Caleb because she thinks they'd make a cute couple, so she shared it with Jacqueline? If so, that makes a huge difference, doesn't it?

Someone who talks all the time is insecure. **Watch.** Keep your eyes open and your ears tuned in to those who talk just to be talking. They barely give the other person room to share anything, and it's obvious they feel **uncomfortable** with silence.

I've known pastors, professors, and friends who all fit into this category. Guess what—it's **exhausting** to be around them. I find myself wanting to scream, "Stop talking for a moment and ask me how I'm doing!"

Someone who's a good listener will **always** have friends. But that's not the only reason we should want to be good listeners. The real reason we strive to understand what others are saying is because we want to be like Jesus. **He truly cared about those around Him.** Ephesians 5:1 tells us to imitate Him. We want to care about others as well. And genuine love means being a good listener.

Susie

FROM GOD:

- ❤ "He who watches over his mouth and his tongue keeps his soul from troubles" (Proverbs 21:23 NLV).
- ❤ "My dear brothers and sisters, always be willing to listen and slow to speak" (James 1:19 NCV).

GO AHEAD—ANSWER:

» How do you feel when someone monopolizes the conversation (left out, angry, interested, bored, etc.)?

» Describe someone you know who always listens to you. Why do you value his or her friendship so much?

» Ask God to bring someone to your mind right now who really needs a listener. Will you be the one who listens?

FROM SUSIE:

Part of being a great listener is also being a good conversationalist. People love to talk about themselves. So learn to ask good questions that help people open up to you.

95.
Go to God first with your problems.

Situation: You've just learned you're getting cut from the track team. You're devastated. You immediately. . .

call your mom.

find your best friend.

start praying.

It's easy to take our **problems** to a friend or a parent before we talk to God about them. After all, an actual human can hug us, cry with us, and pray with us. It's simply natural to seek the comfort of someone close to us.

But King David, **author** of many of the Psalms, knew the importance of going to God first. Oftentimes he cried out to the Lord in frustration, in **fear**, and in confusion. God wants you to do the same. Though it's convenient to quickly turn to a friend, **God** wants to be your first source. He has placed important people in your life to help you **navigate** the storms, but He yearns for you to share your heart with Him.

So why don't we? Why do we tend to go to people first instead of our heavenly Father?

1. We can see people. God is as close as your **breath**. Closer, in fact! He's actually *inside* you. . .if you have accepted Him as your Savior. Yet because we can't see Him in the **flesh**, we tend to think He's far away. This is a **lie** that Satan desperately wants you to believe.

2. We're impatient. We're used to getting things **fast**, and conversation with a friend provides immediate back-and-forth dialogue. Sometimes God seems **slow** in answering. His timing is actually **perfect**, but it often *seems* slow to us.

3. We tend to think God doesn't care. This is another **lie** from Satan—your greatest enemy. Satan wants you to believe that God can't be **bothered** with your problems. After all, He has wars to deal with, angels to think about, tsunamis to end, and hunger to manage. Does He really care if you get asked to the prom?

Yes.

Anything that's important to **you** is important to Him! In fact, there's nothing too **big**—and nothing too small for you to pray about. If it concerns you, it concerns your heavenly Father. Check this out: "Cast all your anxiety on him because he cares for you" (1 Peter 5:7 NIV).

He **wants** you to come to Him with your problems! Here's the proof: "Don't worry about anything; instead, pray about everything; tell God your needs, and don't forget to thank him for his answers" (Philippians 4:6 TLB).

God still wants you to share your problems with those around you; in fact, He has placed **important people** in your life to help you. But He wants you to get in the **habit** of coming to Him first.

He may not answer you in the **timing** or in the way you want Him to, but He will **always** answer your prayers!

Susie

• •

FROM GOD:

- ❤ "Never will I leave you; never will I forsake you" (Hebrews 13:5 NIV).
- ❤ "The LORD is close to the brokenhearted" (Psalm 34:18 NLT).

GO AHEAD—ANSWER:

»—→ Who do you usually go to first when you have a problem?
»—→ At what point do you turn to God during a problem: (First? Last? Whenever I can't find any more friends to talk with? During the middle of the crisis?)
»—→ What kind of difference will it make for you to go to God first and then turn to your friends?

FROM SUSIE:

Friends are often helpful, but I've learned that no one truly understands like Jesus. He understands my feelings, my actions, and my reactions like no one else because He created me. There's an old hymn, "What a Friend We Have in Jesus," that's packed with solid truth!

206

26.
Bake things from scratch.

Before going any further, I feel I must confess that I'm writing this **as I eat a piece of store-bought pie.** Now that I've confessed my hypocrisy, let me tell you why you should bake things from scratch.

- It's much more **delicious** than store-bought pie.
- It's usually **healthier** for you. Or you at least have the option of making it slightly healthier.
- Eating home-baked goods is more **rewarding** than if they're from the grocery store freezer section.
- It builds **memories.** Sometimes messy ones, which you know firsthand if you've **ever accidentally left the lid off the blender before turning it on.** Want to know how many memories I made eating my store-bought pie? None.
- Having to measure ingredients **reinforces** basic math concepts. Buying my pie didn't challenge me mentally at all.
- You can **send some to me!**
- It's fun.
- You can use it as an excuse to invite people over or go drop by and visit your neighbors!
- Did I mention it's more delicious?

Kristin

• •

FROM GOD:

♥ "Show hospitality to one another without grumbling" (1 Peter 4:9 ESV).
♥ "But he would feed you with the finest of the wheat, and with honey from the rock I would satisfy you" (Psalm 81:16 ESV).

GO AHEAD—ANSWER:

»→ Do you enjoy baking or cooking from scratch? Why or why not?
»→ What is your favorite thing to bake or cook?
»→ Can you think of anything you've learned from baking or cooking from scratch that we can learn from spiritually?

FROM KRISTIN:

When you bake from scratch, make sure you don't leave your mess for someone else. Wash your dishes and clean up as you go!

27.
Appreciate the differences in people.

You've probably noticed the **people all around you are different**. Even within your family each person has unique looks, personality, interests, **likes and dislikes**, desires, dreams, and relational needs.

God created each person **precisely** the way **He wanted them**, and we need to appreciate **the differences** in people.

Not everyone has to be good at sports. Or have perfect teeth. Or like green apples. If everyone **looked** the same, played the same **activities**, and ate the exact same **foods**, the world would be incredibly boring.

I am not artistic. I can't draw anything except boxes and stick figures. I once tried creating a comic strip called **The Adventures of Superbox**, where a box wore a cape and flew around saving stick people from box-shaped buildings. **Brilliant, I know.** I showed it to my friend, and she said to stick with writing. **Noted.**

My friend, on the other hand, once drew a picture with her eyes closed and won an entire art contest. And nobody ever even noticed the six hours of shading I did on Superbox!

I'm joking, of course. I only put in four hours of shading.

Okay, being serious now. **My point is this:** don't envy other people's gifts. It wastes precious time you could be spending on nurturing the gifts God's given *you*.

I **love and appreciate** my artistic friends. I love going to museums hearing them explain brushstrokes, patterns, and art history. Likewise, they love and appreciate my ability to throw words into (sometimes) intelligent sentences.

Don't elevate one talent, personality trait, spiritual gift, interest, or physical attribute above another.

Your looks, personality, and talents bring joy to God in a unique way, as do the **looks, personality, and talents of the person standing next to you.**

Kristin

FROM GOD:

- ❤ "What then, brothers? When you come together, each one has a hymn, a lesson, a revelation, a tongue, or an interpretation. Let all things be done for building up" (1 Corinthians 14:26 ESV).
- ❤ "A new commandment I give to you, that you love one another: just as I have loved you, you also are to love one another. By this all people will know that you are my disciples, if you have love for one another" (John 13:34–35 ESV).

GO AHEAD—ANSWER:

»⟶ Do you compare yourself to others? Why?

»⟶ What are some ways you can appreciate the differences in others?

»⟶ Take some time to thank God for creating such a diverse world!

FROM KRISTIN:

I'm incredibly thankful God gave us a variety of interests and passions. It ensures that everyone gets remembered and appreciated!

98.

Own more underwear and socks than you'll actually need.

This chapter is going to be fast and to the point.

Calculate the amount of underwear and socks you think you need. Now double it.

That's the number of socks and underwear you should own.

Here's why:

- At least one-fourth of them will get sock-napped by the laundry gremlin.
- You can **rewear pants and shirts** without getting too smelly. The same can't be said of socks and undies. Therefore, if you have more socks and undies, you can go longer without needing to do laundry.
- Sometimes you'll need to wear multiple pairs of each in a day.
- Socks and underwear get worn out faster than other garments. And they're harder to sew back together. Yes, I've tried.
- If you go on a **long vacation**, you can extend your wardrobe by rewearing shirts and pants, but if you bring enough fresh socks and undies you can feel clean your whole trip!
- If you enjoy hiking or taking long runs, bringing an extra pair of dry socks to change into can make your **excursion more comfortable!**

FROM GOD:

- ♥ "Hear instruction and be wise, and do not neglect it" (Proverbs 8:33 ESV).
- ♥ "An intelligent heart acquires knowledge, and the ear of the wise seeks knowledge" (Proverbs 18:15 ESV).

GO AHEAD—ANSWER:

- »——→ Does having a chapter about socks and underwear seem a little ridiculous?
- »——→ How can we be wise and resourceful with our clothing?
- »——→ So. . .do you own enough?

Kristin

FROM KRISTIN:

I once went on a three-week backpacking trip to Europe. I packed three shirts, three pairs of pants, one dress, and twenty-five pairs each of underwear and socks. And now you know too much.

99.

Know which superpower you'd choose.

"If you got to choose just one superpower, which would it be?"

It's of utmost importance that you **know the answer** to this question. **Someday** you'll be sitting around the table at Thanksgiving—with everyone you've ever met—and someone will call you out in front of *everyone* and ask you the superpower question.

What you say reveals what you value.

For the longest time I thought **invisibility** might be the best power. You could sneak in and out of top-secret meetings and warn good guys about the bad guy's plans.

However, after sitting in airports for a good portion of my life, I've decided that **teleportation** would be superbly helpful in this day and age. You could avoid airports and just show up when needed.

Then I thought **mind reading** might be handy. You could tell when people were getting bored and always win at chess.

These are all fun to think about, but the **best** superpower is one that we can have for real: **the Holy Spirit's power.**

If you've **faith** even as **small as a mustard seed**, you're connected to the Almighty God, the One who has the power to create an entire universe with a single sentence.

You'll have the power to overcome temptation, speak truth in the face of danger, and love those who **hate** you. You may not have a cape, but you'll have a **robe of righteousness.** That's *way* more awesome.

This superpower is better than invisibility, flying, and teleportation combined!

Kristin

. . . .

FROM GOD:

❤ "For God gave us a spirit not of fear but of power and love and self-control" (2 Timothy 1:7 ESV).

❤ "And what is the immeasurable greatness of his power toward us who believe, according to the working of his great might" (Ephesians 1:19 ESV).

GO AHEAD—ANSWER:

»——→ Who's your favorite superhero? Why?

»——→ If you could choose any superpower, what would it be?

»——→ Do you feel confident knowing that you're connected with the Ultimate Power?

FROM KRISTIN:

I love superhero movies because the good guy always wins in the end!

100.
Save your change.

Susie got to talk about how she saves her coins earlier, and now it's my turn! (We're very passionate about this subject.) As much as I can, I use **cash** to pay for things. It makes budgeting easier and helps keep me from overspending.

Very rarely do I actually have the *exact* change. (By the way, every time you pay with exact change a squirrel makes it safely across the street.) When I pay, the cashier gives me back an assortment of dollars and coins. The dollars I stuff in my wallet. My coins usually end up on the bottom of my bag.

One day while deep cleaning my room, bags, and car, I collected and gathered all my spare change into a pile. At the end of the day I counted it. Twenty-three dollars! Not bad for a bunch of pennies, nickels, dimes, and quarters collecting at the bottom of my bag, right?

I decided for a year I'd keep and save my coins. Every couple of days I'd clean out all the change from my bag and car and toss them into an old glass milk jug that I've kept for years. (Or you can do it Susie's way and get a piggy bank. Or maybe you can find a milk jug shaped like a piggy bank. *Please* get one for me if you ever see it. I'll pay you back. . .if I have enough change.) Every month or so I'd separate, count, and put the coins into rolls. At the end of the year I had $183.

A few of my friends and family try and go on a "reunion" trip to Disneyland every year or two. I was able to buy my pass and pitch in to help a friend buy her pass, all because I'd saved my change!

I've since started fresh on a new batch of coins. This time I'm saving for a mission trip to Sudan. So far I have $11. So in about forty years I'll get to go.

Kristin

. . . .

FROM GOD:

- ❤ And a poor widow came and put in two small copper coins, which make a penny. And he called his disciples to him and said to them, 'Truly, I say to you, this poor widow has put in more than all those who are contributing to the offering box' " (Mark 12:42–43 ESV).
- ❤ "Wealth gained hastily will dwindle, but whoever gathers little by little will increase it" (Proverbs 13:11 ESV).

GO AHEAD—ANSWER:

»⟶ Have you ever collected or saved your coins?

»⟶ What can collecting change teach you?

»⟶ Would you like to save up for anything?

FROM KRISTIN:

Since I've started collecting and saving my change, cleaning out my car, room, and bags has become less of a chore and more like a treasure hunt!

101.
Rejoice in the Lord always.
(And again I say, Rejoice!)

What does it mean to rejoice? Check all that apply:

___ a. Laughing until stuff comes out your nose.

___ b. Being glad.

___ c. Feeling ridiculously happy and giddy.

___ d. Showing gratitude.

___ e. Dancing in a public place.

___ f. Displaying joy.

You can actually do and feel and be all of the above when you rejoice, but it all boils down to being joyful because of what God has done for you. It's kind of like counting your blessings. *What? You've never counted your blessings?*

A good time to do this is at the beginning of each year. I try to get alone with God and think back through the year. I ask Him to help me remember the blessings He has given me through the year. Then I thank Him.

I commit the current year to Him, and I ask Him to do in me and through me what I've not yet seen Him do. Then I start watching for Him to reveal Himself in special ways to me.

It's easy to rejoice when things are going well. . .but it's much tougher to rejoice when things are falling apart. How can we rejoice and mean it during the hard times?

Strive not to focus on what's going wrong, but fix your attention, instead, on all that's going right. In other words, thank God for what He's doing in your life right now. Thank Him for the things He has blessed you with in the past. Again . . .counting your blessings.

This is important because: someday when you're feeling all alone, you'll be able to ask Him to remind you of the praises you've given Him, the blessings He has bestowed, and the miracles He has done for you. You'll be in the perfect position for Him to take you back to a place of true thanksgiving. When that happens, you can rejoice no matter what you're currently experiencing.

Susie

FROM GOD:

- ♥ "But may all who seek you rejoice and be glad in you" (Psalm 40:16 NIV).
- ♥ "But I trust in your unfailing love; my heart rejoices in your salvation" (Psalm 13:5 NIV).

GO AHEAD—ANSWER:

»→ What's the last thing you truly rejoiced about?

»→ How can you experience joy in the midst of trials?

»→ Describe someone you admire who is genuinely joyful. What's his or her secret?

FROM SUSIE:

There's a really old hymn called "Count Your Blessings." Google it and read through the verses. Then start counting your blessings!

Sinner's Prayer

So now you've read through our 101 tips for life. Some are pretty lighthearted, others more serious. But nothing is more serious than knowing Jesus Christ personally. If you've never "accepted" Jesus into your life, please consider praying the following prayer. You'll never regret that decision!

DEAR JESUS:

I admit I'm a sinner. I've disobeyed You, and I'm really sorry. Will You forgive me of my sins? I'm placing my faith in You, and I want to live for You the rest of my life. Thank You for loving me enough to die for my sins—and for conquering death and preparing a place for me in heaven with You for all eternity.

I accept Your gift of forgiveness. Please help me to grow closer to You, to fall in love with You, and to obey You. In Your name I pray, Amen.

About the Authors

Kristin is a writer and comedian from Dallas, Texas. She contributes to *Sisterhood Magazine*, a national publication for teen girls, and does stand-up comedy all over the country. She also speaks to teen girls and leads Bible studies for middle and high school girls. www.kristinweberonline.com

Susie speaks forty weeks/weekends out of the year and has written fifty-three books but says this is the only one she's actually read. She's the founding editor of *Sisterhood Magazine*, lives in Bethany, Oklahoma, and is trying to teach Obie and Amos—her two mini Schnauzers—vocabulary words and phrases. She's currently working on, "Stop using my credit card to order things from Animal Planet!" Book Susie to speak at your next event or learn more about her at: SusieShellenberger.com.

Life Can Be Challenging for Teen Girls. . . .

Smart Girl's Guide to Mean Girls, Manicures, and God's Amazing Plan for Me

The Smart Girl's Guide to Mean Girls, Manicures, and God's Amazing Plan for Me melds spiritual and practical advice with humor—a winning combination as teen girls try to navigate the ups and downs of life with grace and confidence. Girls will be encouraged and challenged with sound, biblically based advice equipping them to go deeper in their faith and grow an increasingly intimate relationship with God—plus, they'll encounter some fun, common-sense tips along the way.

Paperback / 978-1-63409-713-0 / $12.99

21 Myths (Even Good) Girls Believe About Sex

21 Myths (Even Good) Girls Believe about Sex uncovers the most believed untruths girls have about dating and sex. With honest, straightforward language Jennifer Strickland shares the myths, the truths, and the practical ways young women can enjoy the pursuit of passion and purity.

Paperback / 978-1-63409-133-6 / $14.99